The **POWER** Series

RED FLAG

Air Combat for the 1990s

Michael Skinner and George Hall

Motorbooks International
Publishers & Wholesalers ®

To Brian Ferguson

First published in 1993 by Motorbooks International Publishers & Wholesalers, PO Box 2, 729 Prospect Avenue, Osceola, WI 54020 USA

Library of Congress Cataloging-in-Publication Data
Skinner, Michael.
    Red Flag/Michael Skinner, George Hall. – –2nd ed.
        p. cm. – – (The Power Series)
    Includes index.
    ISBN 0-87938-759-9
        1. Air warfare. 2. Fighter planes– –United States. 3. War games.
    I. Hall, George (George N.). II. Title. III. Series: Power series (Osceola, Wis.)
    UG630.H323   1993
    358.4'156– –dc20   93-1162

Printed and bound in Hong Kong

On the front cover: F-15 Eagles over an undercast. *James Benson*

On the back cover: An F-15 flashes by in full afterburner. The display for the Red Flag Measuring and Debriefing System records and displays the whole fight so the Players can review their performance after the show.

On the frontispiece: A plane captain (Navy term for crew chief) awaits dawn start-up of his F/A-18 Hornet. *Tom Twomey*

On the title page: A beautifully-painted Adversary F-16C slips back into Nellis after a Red Flag defensive mission. *George Hall*

Contents

Acknowledgments

In the preparation of this new edition, I received help, advice, and hair-raising anecdotes from dozens of people in the know. Thousands of military pilots have enjoyed Red Flag's E-ticket ride, and fortunately they love talking about it. I'll mention only a few; but as the saying goes, the rest of you know who you are. My thanks go to Gen. Chuck Horner, chief architect of our enormously successful air war in the Persian Gulf and one of Red Flag's earliest cheerleaders. Thanks also to Capt. Eric "Neck" Dodson, a Silver Star-bedecked Falcon driver who's experienced both Red Flag and the more realistic version south of Baghdad. And to Red Flag staff officers Col. Jim Henderson, Lt. Col. Murky Waters, Lt. Col. Phil "PT" Finke, Maj. John "Bunky" Barrett, and intel whiz Capt. Heidi Kasel, who gave me up-to-date poop on how things are run in today's desert exercises.

As always, a nod is due to the many helpful and professional public affairs types who the Air Force fields in such profusion. Lots of these folks have helped me with other projects over the years: Col. Ron Sconyers, Capt. Kevin Baggett, Capt. Tom Barth, Capt. Kelly Ann Thompson at Luke AFB in Arizona, and of course Maj. Greg Kreis, Linda Johnsrud, and MSgt. Ron Bloise at Nellis. Bloise was so glad to get rid of me that he up and retired from the Air Force the morning after I left.

Kudos as well for the Rio Hotel and Casino in Las Vegas, my favored hangout when staying in that decidedly strange town. It's new, hot, and very well run; it even has a pool with a real sand beach! Eschew the Strip and try it next time. And no, this is not a paid plug.

The photos in this book were taken on many flights over the vast Nevada ranges during the last dozen years. On my one and only fast-mover hop in a real Red Flag exercise, I was so terrified by the spectacle of seventy jets within Sidewinder range that I could scarcely focus the camera. More relaxed flights in tankers, AWACS, and C-130 bush-beaters yielded the best shots. My thanks to a hundred nameless pilots for pretty posing and shit-hot flying.

An Eagle driver checks his five o'clock for the bad guys. George Hall

George Hall
Tiburon, California
October 1992

Foreword

If, as the Duke of Wellington said, the battle of Waterloo was won on the playing fields of Eton, then certainly the Gulf War—history's most effective air campaign—was won over the deserts of northern Nevada, in the world's most realistic war game, Red Flag.

Commenced a decade and a half before Desert Storm, Red Flag projected Saddam's war to an eerie degree: an interlocking network of MiGs, missiles, guns, and radars, woven together Soviet style and spread out over a seemingly endless and empty desert. That was the puzzle presented to an entire generation of Western pilots who earned their spurs in the Nellis range wars. And if they had never found the solution, Desert Storm would have had a much different, and less satisfactory conclusion.

Red Flag was just hitting its stride when George Hall and I flew to Nellis to research the original book. That was almost a decade ago; quite an exciting time to be hanging around the ramp. The entire American military was undergoing a renaissance then: new weapons, new tactics, new attitude. Red Flag meant the latest jets—*Eagles! Falcons! Warthogs!*—as well as the brilliant Aggressor birds found nowhere else, in their rare Russ-

An Eagle two-ship flies a high-altitude CAP over atypical cloud deck. George Hall

ian plumage: *Lizards, Grapes, Gomers, Ghosts.* By the light of the Vegas Strip, over the moonscape of the Great Basin, our plucky boys set out to relearn the art and science of air combat, their only hope against the cold precision and sheer numbers of the Soviet Military Machine.

Now, ten years later, it's hard to comprehend how quickly and how completely everything has changed. The Soviet Union—that Evil Empire, that Military Monolith—self-destructed, seemingly overnight, and with it went the rationale for virtually the entire US defense build-up. Red Flag was never the same, certainly. No more MiG-5 jockeys babbling pidgin Russian, no more documents classified Cyrillic, no more red stars on the toilet seats in the Aggressor's men's room.

Not soon after that, Desert Storm broke. Although its political significance can perhaps be debated, its military efficacy cannot. It was a complete rout, a triumph of Western military art so great it even took the Pentagon by surprise. Red Flag planners were no doubt ecstatic to see that fifteen years of training and simulation had not been wasted (validation was a question that had nagged Red Flag since its inception). But no one could have seen more clearly than Air Force strategic thinkers that Desert Storm was something of a fluke: the right war, in the right place, at the right time, against the right kind of enemy.

Military triumph it was, and we will never see the likes of it again.

It's been said that only defeated generals learn from past battles; the victorious merely prepare to fight the last war over again. Red Flag, to its credit, has moved beyond Desert Storm, and is learning and teaching the lessons of the next air war, over a more unsettled, though no less dangerous, world. How it's going about that is the subject of this updated book.

I have not been back to Nellis since 1983. George Hall practically lives there. And why not? His business, after all, is photographing the latest and greatest in tactical aviation, and there's no better place to do that than Nellis Air Force Base, Nevada. It's been said that if you sat long enough in the lobby of the Peabody Hotel in Memphis, Tennessee, eventually you'd meet everybody worth meeting in the South. Nellis is like that for airplanes.

This update, then, is his work. I've limited myself to correcting some youthful excesses and adding bits here and there gleaned from an ensuing decade of tail spotting, hangar flying, and fighter bar hopping. But if the reader

Home of The Fighter Pilot. Rare indeed is the American combat aviator who has never visited Nellis AFB. George Hall

Eagles fly CAP over a low-lying sun.

can't tell where I leave off and George begins, then that's fine with me.

I never expected this book to live this long. At any rate, I thought I had retired from this business. There was, I thought, a finite number of things you could say about airplanes, and after a half-dozen books and countless magazine articles, I'd said them all. But not too long ago, I was at another air show, staring open-mouthed at a pair of the last surviving F-4s. They screamed in with fantastic grace, smudging the blue sky gray at full mili-tary power, sun diamonding off the canopy. Their roar met mine at the top of my throat, flaps and stabilators fluttering, four gray helmets nodding toward me as they arced out of sight towing a scream, then silence, and then I knew I had not ever even gotten close to what flying fighters is really like. And I knew I never would. No one ever could.

Michael Skinner
Marietta, Georgia
January 1993

Chapter 1

Student Gap

North of the neon furnaces and gambling pits of Las Vegas is a bigger game played for higher stakes. In this strange game there is no score, but there are winners and losers. The winners gain nothing but the chance to play again; the losers can lose everything. The game is called Red Flag, and it is strictly for the highest rollers of all.

Head north out of Vegas, past the sprawling Nellis Air Force Base ten miles from town, past where the highway turns prudently away from the Air Force's live bombing ranges, and you will come to a cut between two hard, brown mountains. Earthlings call this pass, where State Highway 93 intersects the 115th meridian, the Pahroc Summit. But it has another name.

If you leave your air-conditioned rental car and scramble out among the creosote and the blackbrush, you'll soon wish you hadn't. The heat will assault you, the glare will blind you, but it is the desolation, the sheer aloneness of the place, that will drive you to the edge. When the hot winds die there is no sound, no sound at all, save for the occasional humming of a car sensibly leaving the middle of nowhere.

An F-15 Eagle lights the pipes for a dusk takeoff. Red Flag will soon have a larger night-fighting component. George Hall

Two Navy Hornets roll "in hot" with inert Mark 82 bombs. Jet 400 carries a data transmission pod on his right wing-tip station. Robert Lawson

But if you stay out here long enough, something will happen. You will feel it long before you see it—a vague premonition, a sense of thunder from the east. If it's your normal CAVU (Clear Air, Visibility Unlimited) Nevada day—quartz-clear and hundred-mile viz—you might even see it coming: a black dot crawling over the shimmer of the highway as it runs east to the little town of Caliente. Immediately, the dot swells and sprouts wings. It is upon you in an instant, a smoking, hulking beast scorching across the desert at 500 knots easy. Before your mind can categorize and dismiss it as an Air Force F-111F Aardvark fighter-bomber, there is an initial sense of awe and terror. With its pivoting wings swept back, the aircraft resembles an ancient pterodactyl, the huge, leather-wing monster that haunted this desert a million years ago. When that enormous shadow falls across you, it is easy to feel the ancient fight-or-flight impulse of the caveman. The feeling clutches at your throat and grips you in its dark power. The moment is gone in a heartbeat, but the memory will never leave.

As quickly as it appeared, the jet is gone. The pterodactyl's shadow scuttles over the brown scrub and folds itself up Mount Irish. The radar in its drooping black snout nods and swivels on its gimbals, searching for the rocks

Desert Storm vet "Jester" Jessurd taxis his Falcon on the Nellis tarmac prior to a Red Flag mission.
Lans Stout

14

and mountains in its path. The F-111 shoots the pass low and fast, barely a hundred feet above the weeds.

Like the sidewinder, another citizen of the desert floor, for every F-111 you see, there are dozens of planes you don't. High above your head, up where the sky curves into indigo, there's a constant parade of airpower over the Pahroc Summit. Just about every kind of aircraft from every branch of the free world's flying services has overflown that coordinate. They call it Student Gap. It's where the game begins, where the Players cross the inbounds marker, Checkpoint Charlie, on the way to Redland. It's the start of the Red Flag world,

and the closest most of us will get to the Big Game.

From here on in, the pilots are on their own, fair game for the fake MiGs and simulated missile batteries that lie in wait for the unprepared. When they push the Gap, the aircrews are as close to war as anyone would want to get. Some careless or unlucky pilots will "die." Some could die for real, as others have before. There are strict safety rules, but no rules can remove completely the danger involved in high-Mach jousting, in aircraft buzzing around each other like supersonic dragonflies, in dragging live bombs so low their shadows are tucked beneath them.

Venezuelan Brig. Gen. Juan Paredes starts up on the foreign visitors' ramp during Red Flag 92-4.
George Hall

A Venezuelan crew chief stays in touch with maintenance control as four of his F-16As fire up for a Red Flag mission. George Hall

This inherent danger is what Red Flag is all about: an introduction to life at the edge for the young tigers. Red Flag may not be a *precise* simulation of today's air war. How could it be? Nevertheless, the pressure of war is there—nothing simulated about that.

"There's a tremendous amount of pressure here," says a pilot taking part in Red Flag for the first time. "You sense it when you walk in the front door. Everyone's under the gun."

"It's a learning situation," says an F-15 driver. "You can't always back off. There's going to be times when you're thrust into a situation and they say, "Hey, react!""

"If you compare Red Flag with war, then sure, the violence level is much, much lower," says a Red Flag staffer. "But for the guy who's never been in combat, it's a hell of an accurate taste. When he comes to Red Flag he's a very, very busy young man."

An F-15 pilot, interviewed on Cable News Network (CNN) after a Desert Storm mission, actually commented, "With the big exception of people shooting at you, these missions are easier than the ones we flew at Red Flag."

That's what Red Flag is all about, to give the young tactical pilot combat experience in the absence of combat. Maybe you can't build an exact replica of a Russian-designed integrated air defense system in the Nevada desert (although you can try); but you *can* simulate the disorientation of combat, the high-Mach version of Von Clauswitz's *Fog of War,* the sensory overload that's often more dangerous to inexperienced pilots than all the anti-aircraft artillery (AAA), surface-to-air missiles (SAMs), and MiGs ever built. To the young hotshots who think they have the juice, Red Flag gives new meaning to the term "pressurized cockpit."

Red Flag is referred to as a game, but it's more like a sport, where teamwork and timing count more than mere athletic ability. It is event-oriented training, a problem with as many solutions as there are Players. It is definitely not an inspection or evaluation, nor is it a test, but rather a place to be tested. It is an opportunity for new pilots to make some rookie mistakes and for veterans to try something new in a realistic but nonlethal environment. It is a place for the people who operate the Air Force's diverse, but increasingly interdependent, weapons systems to meet, argue, laugh, think, drink, and train with one another. Most important, it is a chance for warriors to get wartime experience without risk.

"We try not to evaluate people at Red Flag. We don't test them, we don't give them check rides, and we don't let wings use Red Flag as some kind of ORI [Operational Readiness Inspection]. No evaluations," says the Red Flag commanding officer (CO). "It's a learning program, and we don't want them under the pressure of a test because, invariably, people who are being tested don't learn as well. It's like a golfer choosing between his sure-thing shot as opposed to the one he thinks he *might* be able to pull off. We want people to train here, not fall back on that sure-thing shot."

Like most of the US Air Force's newer training programs, Red Flag is an outgrowth of the Air Force's poor showing in the Vietnam

War. One of the few good things to have come out of that bad war was the rediscovery of some old rules of air combat, rules the United States had long forgotten and had to relearn very painfully in the skies over Route Pack Six (a targeting corridor over Hanoi and Haiphong).

Most pertinent to Red Flag was the axiom that a pilot's chances for survival, as well as his combat effectiveness, rise dramatically in relation to the number of combat missions he flies. It doesn't take many missions—ten seems to be the optimum number; after that, diminishing returns set in, and the pilot is about as good as he's going to get.

The trick was providing inexperienced pilots with ten missions' worth of experience without exposing them to actual combat. The Air Force's post-Vietnam emphasis on realistic training programs had already produced a simulated enemy force, the Aggressors, and a battlefield studded with threats and targets on the Nellis AFB range. What was needed was a way to tie it all together, to use those

Race-tracking at altitudes above 40,000 feet, the E-3A Sentry AWACS controls the fight in concert with *the referees in the BLACKJACK range facility.*
James Benson

assets to give young American pilots a head start in air combat. The solution was Red Flag, and the man with the plan was Richard M. "Moody" Suter.

"Moody was the kind of guy who would aggressively pursue what everybody knew to be good ideas," says a past Red Flag CO. "These were not, by any stretch of the imagination, ideas unique to Moody Suter. But what he did was travel the world and take notes at fighter-pilot bars; he'd literally write stuff down on bar napkins. As he would visit air bases, both during and after the Vietnam War, he would compile lists of ideas from the people he'd talk to. And there was one common thread: we didn't go far enough in our training programs to prepare for war-fighting. That discontinuity between what we did in peacetime and wartime was very costly."

It wasn't that Air Force training was bad; it just didn't go far enough. It took pilots right up to the point of realistic air combat training and then left them hanging. Even worse, after initial training the pilots were relegated to "flying around the flagpole," concerned with only logging the required number of flight hours with scarcely a thought to the mission. During a period in the 1960s, one "fighter"

Full of gas, an F-111F Aardvark falls away from its tanker in Track 641. George Hall

squadron in England did not fly a single air-to-air training mission for three years. Their experience, or lack of it, was not unique. And as the Air Force moved into complex multi-role aircraft like the F-4 Phantom, multi-role aircrews were expected to be proficient in everything from dogfights to dropping the Big One. There was barely enough time to stay current, much less get really good at anything.

"In 1975, we started looking hard at tactical fighter and attack training to find out what was missing," says the former Red Flag skipper. "The answer we found was that nothing was really missing; we just didn't go nearly far enough. We stopped at too low a proficiency level, in terms of the broad, dynamic types of decisions that you would have to make in combat. We were stopping way too short."

The skipper continues: "So we set out, then, to structure a flying training program that didn't fundamentally change what we had done in the past, but added an extension to it, to go from undergraduate level to grad school and doctorate level."

Moody Suter got the ear of Gen. Robert Dixon, a fighter jock's fighter jock who was then head of the Tactical Air Command (TAC). General Dixon knew a good idea when he heard one (he was later awarded the Collier

Canadian CF-18 chases two Dutch F-16As over the swamps north of CFB Cold Lake, home of Maple Flag exercises. John McQuarrie

Trophy for establishing Red Flag). The first Red Flag was held three months later, on the Nellis range, in November 1975.

The long-since-retired General Dixon was no doubt delighted to see, when he paid a visit to Red Flag country in early 1992, that today's exercises are similar to that first set-to. The basics, which have remained the same, consist of the following: The schedule is holding at six exercises per year, each of six weeks' duration. (One is a Green Flag, and one is a Maple Flag. The staff is also experimenting with a Night Flag concept. More on those variants later.) Some people stay at Nellis for the entire six

weeks, but most units are rotated every two weeks. Thus, each mini-war lasts ten flying days with weekends off (after all, we're talking Las Vegas). The Players fly two missions per day, the first being a familiarization hop to orient the newcomer to the Nellis facility.

A scenario is written by the Red Flag intelligence types concerning the imminent hostilities between "Red," the bad guys who live on the western side of the Nellis range, and "Blue," the coalition good guys defending the neighboring eastern part of the range.

The Blue forces consist of everything from fighters and strikers to heavy bombers and

Summer in Cold Lake isn't too bad; Canadians mumble something about ten months of winter and two months of lousy sledding. Here an England- *based Aardvark's radar antenna is being lubricated.* James Benson

A huge B-52 leaves Nellis for a run through the bombing ranges. Heavy bombers now stage from Nellis during Red Flags, instead of making long cross-country flights from their Midwest bases. George Hall

A Venezuelan Falcon joins the takeoff line-up during Red Flag 92-4. On occasion forty jets will clog the run-up area waiting to take the active runways. George Hall

A French Armee de l' Aire pilot conveys a mainte- nance "gripe" to his crew chief. The French have spent decades serving in various African outposts, and they obviously know how to dress for the desert. George Hall

cialties began intruding in the 1980s, and the exercises started to take on different personal- ities: strike/attack scenarios with lots of cold steel on target; close air support wars with swarms of A-10s, Army helicopters, and for- ward air control from the ground; a heavy em- phasis on airborne electronics, with major radar jamming, radio intel gathering, and pos- itive Airborne Warning and Control System (AWACS) control. These latter scenarios have been deemed so important that they've been given their own name, Green Flag, after the phosphorescent glow of the radar screen. At present, one Green Flag is staged each year, and the fighters and attackers are supple- mented by jammers like the EF-111 Raven, the anti-SAM Wild Weasels, secretive RC-135 Rivet Joint airborne listening posts, and E-2 or E-3 AWACS command-and-control planes. And with the stunning nocturnal successes over Iraq came a new awareness of the impor- tance of training in the dark. Hence, the latest twist at Nellis: Night Flag, with half of all missions blasting off after sunset. From now on, at least two Red Flags per year will have a big night-fighting element.

Flag exercises are not short-notice deploy- ment drills. The Players will know at least a year in advance that they're on the schedule. A surprise invitation to come to Nellis wouldn't serve any real purpose other than to embarrass the grossly unprepared. That would violate one of the unwritten rules of Red Flag, which is to take advantage of every action, every deployment, and learn some- thing from it.

"There are two elements of combat," says a Red Flag officer. "For us in the United States, getting there is at least half of the problem. Fighting when you get there is going to grab the headlines, but the fundamental issue is that you must be able to get there. So there is a small, but very important part of Red Flag dedicated to the deployment phase.

"Before they [the Players] come to Red Flag, they have to make sure all minor main- tenance write-ups are fixed, and all the time- change maintenance requirements are taken

electronic-warfare birds. In addition, the Blue side might enlist all manner of partners: Navy and Marine Corps assets, strategic bombers from the newly formed Air Combat Command (these are former Strategic Air Command planes), North Atlantic Treaty Organization (NATO) Players, allies from the Middle East, and the excellent French Armee de L'Air. Even small air forces from the likes of Singa- pore, Argentina, and Venezuela have been known to bring well-flown Mirages and F-16s to the defense of the beloved Blueland. The Reds are headed up by a group of former Ag- gressor pilots on the Red Flag staff who fly strangely camouflaged F-16Cs. They also en- list the aid of several other fighter units, fly- ing mostly F-15s and F-16s, to take on the good guys over the range.

Red Flag exercises vary widely in empha- sis. In the early days the focus was on air-to- air jousting; all else was rubbish, as Baron Von Richtofen was fond of saying. Other spe-

care of on their jets. When they're loading the cargo planes, they've literally got to put max gross weight on every aircraft, no cubic feet wasted. We also process the people as if we're going to war. There's no difference, as far as the processing goes—the shots and the paperwork—whether they're turning left and going to Nellis or turning right and going to Europe."

Nor are the pilots immune to the rigors of mock deployment. Used to leisurely stopovers on their way cross-country, Red Flag Players are obliged to make the trip to Nellis all at once, wearing poopy suits (water survival long-distance flight gear) and following

tankers for as much as fourteen hours at a stretch.

"We want it to hurt," says Red Flag's vice commander, "because it's going to hurt when you have to turn around and go the other direction for ten or twelve hours."

Red Flag is administrated by the innocuously named 414th Composite Training Squadron, an element of the Tactics and Weapons Center at Nellis. All this terminology is new for 1992, as is the name of Red Flag's big daddy, the Air Combat Command. With the disappearance of the Strategic Air Command (SAC) after forty years of Cold War fighting, the former Tactical Air Command

A Cannon AFB-based F-111 prepares to taxi on the Red Flag line. Note the side-by-side seating for the *two-man crew, with bombardier-navigator on right.* George Hall

(read fighters) has been combined with SAC's bomber assets and a goodly chunk of its tankers as well. The rest of the tankers are now controlled by the new 1990s version of the Military Airlift Command (MAC), now called the Air Mobility Command.

Several other exercises around the world attempt to graft the Red Flag experience onto other environments. As mentioned, one Red Flag per year is held jointly with flying elements of the Canadian armed forces. Called Maple Flag, this exercise takes place over ranges near Canadian Forces Base (CFB) Cold Lake, Alberta, 200 miles north of Edmonton and miles from anything else. The big Cana-

dian ranges are nowhere near as fully instrumented and threat-studded as the Red Flag facility; there is no live bomb-dropping permitted at Maple Flag, either. The main benefit has been the look of the terrain around Cold Lake. Way back when we were worried about defending Europe, Maple Flag offered green pine forests, lots of snow on the ground, and typically horrible European-style flying weather—quite a switch from the heat, light-colored sand, and CAVU conditions that typify Nellis (when *Canadians* name a place Cold Lake, you know you're in trouble).

Another Red Flag clone is Cope Thunder, put on annually by the Pacific Air Forces and

A Fulcrum paint scheme on an Adversary F-16C blends with the salt ponds below Tanker Track 625 west of the range. George Hall

flown—until recently—out of Clark AFB in the Philippines. But local politics and Mount Pinatubo have conspired to move the American military out of its Philippine bases, and Cope Thunder off the schedule. There's talk of continuing the exercise out of Hickam AFB in Honolulu, but in the interim, Cope Thunder has found a home in the two principal Alaska AFBs—Elmendorf in Anchorage and Eielson in subarctic Fairbanks.

Europe has never mounted an exercise equivalent to Red Flag; restrictions on tactical military flying there make it hardly worth the trouble. Large-scale ground exercises, such as the annual Reforger maneuvers, have always had limited aerial components, but even these are now mere shadows of the former Gotterdamerung glory. American air and ground forces in Europe will continue to wither almost to nothing in the remaining years of the century, barring some unimaginable military crisis in that region.

The Air National Guard employs Red Flag training techniques in several of its annual Sentry exercises. The one with the hottest rep is Sentry Eagle, held each June at the small Kingsley Field in Klamath Falls, Oregon. The resident unit, the 114th Fighter Training Squadron (FTS), is the training school for the Guard's air-defense F-16As; these are the only Falcons in the Air Force inventory configured to carry the AIM-7 Sparrow radar-guided missile. Sentry Eagle spans just one long weekend, but its five hops offer the biggest fighter furballs this side of the Marianas Turkey Shoot, with upwards of sixty fighters and attack jets—active Air Force, Guard, Navy, Marines, and Canadians—staging from Kingsley's one runway (a feat in itself) and going at it in huge Red-Blue fights over central Washington.

A quick word about the Navy's TOPGUN program, which is often compared, incorrectly, with Red Flag. Red Flag is a mock war, with bad guys, objectives, and a beginning, middle, and end. TOPGUN is a school, something of a postgraduate course in Navy fighter weapons, tactics, and fleet doctrine. TOPGUN students fly plenty of engagements against their instructors, a la Maverick vs. Viper in the movie, but they spend more time in the classroom than in flight. TOPGUN is actually more analogous to the Air Force Fighter Weapons School at Nellis. The intent is that the students of both schools will return to their units to impart what they've learned. Like Red Flag, TOPGUN grew out of the less-than-terrific results achieved by Navy fighter pilots in Vietnam.

The grandfather of TOPGUN was Navy Capt. Frank Ault who, like Moody Suter, concluded that good results would spring from lots of high-pressure practice against shit-hot dissimilar adversaries and simulated threats on the ground.

Red Flag is always a big, big exercise, with as many as thirty separate units flying in to take part. Fairly typical is Red Flag 92-4 (the fourth scheduled exercise for 1992). Here are the Players, and quite a swath they cut on the gigantic Nellis ramp:

Blue Offensive Counter-Air:
325th Fighter Wing, six F-15As, Tyndall AFB, Florida
33rd Fighter Wing, six F-15Cs, Eglin AFB, Florida
57th Fighter Squadron, six F-15Cs, Keflavik NS, Iceland

Red Defensive Counter-Air:
414th Composite Training Squadron, four F-16Cs, Nellis AFB, Nevada
56th Fighter Wing, six F-16Cs, MacDill AFB, Florida
58th Fighter Wing, six F-16Cs, Luke AFB, Arizona
86th Fighter Wing, ten F-16Cs, Ramstein AB, Germany

Interdiction Strikers:
2nd Weapons Group, two B-52Gs, Barksdale AFB, Louisiana
27th Fighter Wing, eight F-111Es, Cannon AFB, New Mexico
363rd Fighter Wing, six F-16Cs, Shaw AFB, South Carolina
(Operating from the auxilary field at Indian Springs)

384th Weapons Group, three B-1Bs, Mc-Connell AFB, Kansas

58th Fighter Wing, six F-15Es, Luke AFB, Arizona

96th Weapons Group, three B-1Bs, Dyess AFB, Texas

2/3 Escadron de Chasse, eight Mirage 2000s, Dijon, France

Grupo 16, five F-16As, Maracaibo, Venezuela

Tactical Reconnaissance:

152nd Reconnaissance Group, four RF-4Cs, Nevada Air Guard, Reno, Nevada

Tactical Airlift:

314th Air Mobility Wing, four C-130s, Little Rock AFB, Arkansas

317th Air Mobility Wing, four C-130s, Pope AFB, North Carolina

CIET 34, two C-160s, Toulouse, France

Airborne Command and Control:

552nd Airborne Control Wing, two E-3Bs, Tinker AFB, Oklahoma

Electronic Countermeasures:

355th Weapons Group, two EC-130, Davis-Monthan AFB, Arizona

Nonflying Support:

4th Marine LAAM Battalion, HAWK missiles, Fresno, California

5th Army Special Forces Group, search and rescue techniques, Fort Campbell, Kentucky

Two-thirds of Red Flag's gaggle of Adversary fighters, left over from the Aggressor squadrons that disbanded in 1990. Clearly visible are the Flogger (desert camo) and Fulcrum (air superiority) paint schemes. George Hall

7th Army Special Forces Group, escape and evasion techniques, Fort Bragg, North Carolina

Some of these units operated out of Nellis for the entire six weeks of the exercise, while others stayed for only one or two two-week periods. The French and Venezuelan contingents kept their jets on hand for the whole exercise, but rotated large numbers of pilots and maintenance people through Las Vegas to spread out the unique Red Flag experience as much as possible. This meant their pilots (and backseat bombardiers, in the case of the Mirage 2000-N strikers) got only five Red Flag hops apiece, prompting lots of moaning and groaning in several languages; fighter pilots the world around hate hanging out in the ready room while their buddies get the rides.

In every Red Flag exercise, one squadron or wing is designated the Core Unit for the six-week duration. This unit is the character driver for the whole war; it gets to decide what form the exercise will take and what sorts of tactics and techniques will be emphasized. In Red Flag 92-4 the Core Unit was a near-squadron of eight F-111E Aardvarks out of Cannon AFB in Clovis, New Mexico. They drove the bus for every one of the fifty-seven missions (the optimum is two per day or ten per week for six weeks, but a few got scrubbed

A Russian Su-27 Flanker, although big for a fighter, has awesome aerodynamic performance and modern digital radar systems. Katsuhiko Tokunaga

due to rare heavy rains). And since the Aardvark is, despite its meaningless F designation, a strike bomber rather than a fighter, the accent was on low-level and mid-altitude ground attack—as the mud-movers like to say, "bombs on target."

Everyone got into the act: B-1s and B-52s, F-15E Strike Eagles, F-16Cs (a superb bomber despite a limited carrying capacity), and of course the big 'Varks. Even the French purchased a bunch of American Mark 84 iron bombs so they could rearrange some north Las Vegas real estate with their very capable Mirage 2000-N fighter-bombers.

Opposing all this mayhem was the Red counter-air force, led by the Adversary Tactics Division of the 414th Composite Training Squadron, Red Flag's administrative unit. A dozen or so Red Flag staff officers fly these Red missions, simulating enemy tactics and

A Russian-built MiG-29 Fulcrum in Czechoslovak livery. This excellent 1980s-technology jet is currently flown by some thirty air forces around the world. Katsuhiko Tokunaga

showing the other Red Players, usually F-16s, how to do likewise. The Adversary Tactics Division is all that remains of the once-feared 64th and 65th Aggressor Squadrons that shaped Red Flag tactical doctrine until the eve of the Gulf War. As with so many other things that faded away with the decade of the 1980s, it was money, or rather the lack of same, that doomed the Aggressors.

The current-day Red Flag adversaries managed to keep hold of nine former Aggressor jets; the rest were shifted to other duties when the squadrons were disbanded in 1990. The adversary jets, four of which usually lead the Red counter-air forces on each Red Flag mission, are current F-16C Falcons, delivered in 1986.

Unlike the Navy's F-16N adversary birds, which were stripped of all excess weight and systems to make them into unbeatable dogfighters, the Air Force Aggressor jets are off-the-shelf C-models complete with full-up radar, M-61 rotary cannon, and all war-fighting software for the computerized flight and weapons controls. They differ from wing airplanes in only one respect: all are painted in weird and wonderful camouflage schemes borrowed from various modern Russian-built fighters. The prettiest carry the blue-green-grey pattern seen on the MiG-29 Fulcrum. The larger and more capable Su-27 Flanker usually carries the same scheme, but with a shiny black nose radome. Some of the Red Flag jets will soon carry this added touch of realism. Four others are painted in brown desert camouflage of the type seen on the older MiG-23 Flogger.

"We want to paint them all in the Fulcrum scheme," says Maj. John "Bunky" Barrett, the man who had the dubious distinction of flying the very last Aggressor hop before the 64th and 65th disappeared. "That's the jet we're simulating these days. There are still lots of older Russian fighters around, but the Fulcrum is the most serious threat. It's quite a good jet—not sensational, but quite good. And the Russians are so hard up for cash that they're selling them to absolutely anyone with

the dough. We'll be seeing them all over the world, and if a decent pilot climbs into one, look out. Realistically, that doesn't happen much."

"We're the keeper of the Gomer flame," says Barrett. (The word "Gomer" for flying bad guy cropped up over North Vietnam, and its origin is unclear.) "That was great training, and the units just aren't getting it these days. None of them are getting enough DACT [Dissimilar Air Combat Training], if you ask me. Here at Red Flag we use the building block approach in our engagements. We don't beat them to death in the first engagements; we start a little easy and let them work up their skills. One problem in simulating Russian tactics in the Fulcrum is that the F-16 is such a vastly superior jet. The Russian air-to-air missiles aren't great, and the radar in the MiG-29 is nothing compared to the system we've got. For instance, we have a track-while-scanning mode that lets us keep tabs on ten different targets to the front without painting any of them. In other words, no warning on his RHAW [Radar Homing and Warning] receiver. We can't use that because the MiG doesn't have that capability. So we use single-target track, lock him up the old way, and light up his RHAW gear."

Barrett continues: "These guys flying with us from Ramstein for this Red Flag, they have the new AMRAAM [Advanced Medium-Range Air-to-Air Missile]—it's an awesome fire-and-forget missile. But we leave that out of our Red Flag scenarios too, because the Fulcrum doesn't carry anything in the same room with that missile. Of course, if we let fly with a bunch of max-range AMRAAMs, there wouldn't be much of a fight that day. You have to remind yourself that you're trying to keep it competitive, to maximize the training. So we limit it to rear-quarter Sidewinders, or the Russian AA-10 missile."

But the big force multiplier for the Red side isn't with them in the sky. It's the myriad Black Trash scattered over the desert floor below the strikers—electronically simulated guns, SAMs, and squealing threat radars by

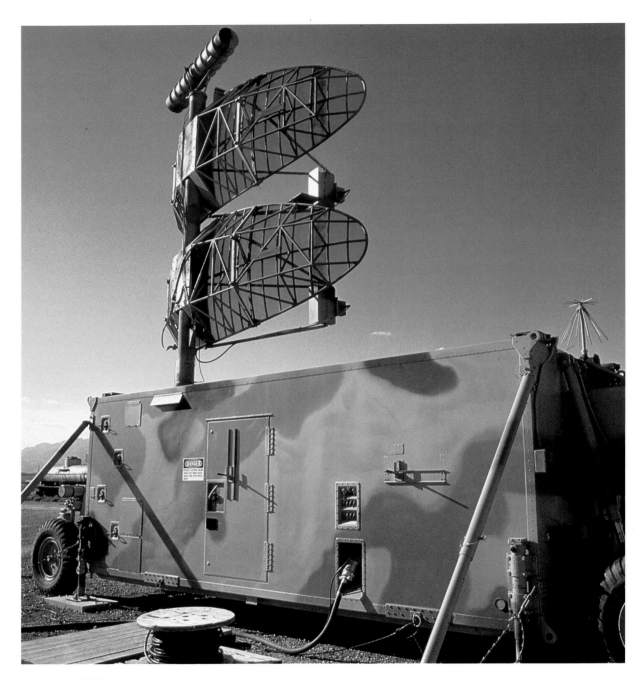

*A mobile SAM radar unit in position to generate
electronic threats on the Nellis range.* George Hall

the score. These nightmare gadgets are operated by skilled civilian threat-mongers who spend long days in the colossal desert heat taking electronic pot-shots at the Blue attackers. It's not enough to check six for enemy fighters out to interrupt the bomb run; the interdiction jets also must defeat the ground threats if they are to take out their targets and return to fight again. This means a whole bag of tricks mixed with perfect timing: violent jinking maneuvers, electronic countermeasures (ECMs), chaff or flares, terrain masking (also known as "groveling in the weeds"), and, of course, max speed, stealth, and surprise.

Occasionally, the range people will mix in some real threats along with the simulators around the targets. In Red Flag 92-4 some Marine reservists from Fresno brought in a HAWK (Homing All the Way Killer) SAM battery; to heighten the realism they moved it around the desert every day. The HAWK has been around for quite a while, but it's still one of the most dreaded of all antiair missile systems. It's guided from the ground by radar, and it's a hard missile to spoof. Like its namesake, it pops up high and makes its attack from above and behind. And this is no shoulder-fired pipsqueak: it's as big and heavy as a Harley-Davidson, and it will be doing about Mach 4 when it hits. Worse still, it's been sold for years on various grey and black markets to at least fifty different countries, including just about everyone in the Middle East. The Iraqis even have a few, but fortunately they've demonstrated no ability to employ them properly.

The Patriot of Gulf War fame is a far more sophisticated and deadly ground-to-air missile system, also built, like the HAWK, by Raytheon. If the Patriot can muster the electronic smarts to find and destroy a supersonic missile like the Scud, one can only imagine how it could handle, say, a great big F-111 doing 450 knots. Army Patriot crews have not yet visited the Nellis ranges during Red Flag, but they've been invited and they are expected to participate in the future.

Now that we've gotten the basics on how Red Flag works, let's acquaint ourselves with the neighborhood. When the Players come to Red Flag, their first mission is always a familiarization ride called a "fam hop"—a half-speed tour of the pattern and the Nellis ranges to get a good look at geography that had been, up to then, just scratches on a map. Sounds like a good idea; let's go on a little fam hop ourselves.

A Marine HAWK (Homing All-The-Way Killer) battery sets up for action in the desert north of Nellis. The half-ton missiles are radar-controlled from the ground, and they can achieve Mach 4 speeds. George Hall

Chapter 2

Fam Hop

Las Vegas is Spanish for "the meadows," a strange name for a place that, as one journalist put it, "could not support the merest form of vegetable life without a massive influx of Teamster funds." When there is wind, it is like dragon's breath. The soil is hard-packed and dry as chalk. Sharp, blue mountains ring the city, as if Las Vegas itself and everyone in it were caught in a giant bear trap, a leg in each jaw, and one step outside would shut that trap forever.

If Vegas seems inhospitable, it is a verdant paradise compared to the country around it. Nevada is the driest of all states. Out here they don't talk about how big a body of water is, just whether it's "permanent." The Great Basin, the vast desert and scrubland north of the city where the Red Flaggers roam, is a curious juxtaposition of the relentless horizontal and the sudden vertical. There are ninety different mountain ranges in the Great Basin, and in between them there is nothing at all.

There *is* life out there; however, most of it is low and scaly: leopard lizards, horned toads, gopher snakes, desert iguanas, spiny lizards, bull snakes, king snakes, Great Basin rattlers, sidewinders, and tarantulas. But there are some surprises as well. The Great Basin is home for the largest water-bird wildlife refuge in America. Mountain lions skulk along the ridges. There are also cattle, raised by ranchers on land leased from the US Bureau of Land Management.

And there are even wild mustangs, at least 5,000 of them, living off the cheatgrass brome—"bronco grass"—a Mediterranean export that unfortunately causes many prairie fires out on the range. The mustangs elude periodic attempts to round them up. They like it out there around Grass Spring Canyon and have enough horse sense to stay out from under the falling Mark 82s. "We've seen dead horses, but never one killed by a bomb," says a range officer.

The rest of the landscape is all scrubgrass and brush: mesquite, yucca, blackbrush, Joshua trees, creosote bush, and sagebrush. No doubt about it, it's Wile E. Coyote country, and a hell of a place for Bugsy Siegel to have positioned America's Pleasure Dome. How did Las Vegas wind up here in the middle of nowhere?

By accident. Las Vegas was built in a salvo of booms. When Nevada was granted statehood in 1864, only the fifty or so Indians and miners who worked the valley were here to greet the travelers from the Rockies as they stopped at the oasis on their way to southern California. But boom after boom of urban alchemists swept the valley—first silver, then

A Strike Eagle of the Fighter Weapons School blasts out of Nellis on a training sortie. George Hall

The new Marine F/A-18D Strike Hornet is an all-weather bomber version that is now replacing the USMC's A-6 Intruders in the heavy attack role. Joe Towers

gold, then the railroad, then the giant Boulder Dam project in the 1930s. Legalized gambling played a big part, of course. So did the sonic boom of the US Air Force.

The flyboys arrived in the form of the Army Air Corps, on January 25, 1941, when the mayor of Las Vegas signed over to the US Army the land that would eventually become Nellis Air Force Base. It really wasn't all that much, just a dirt runway, a water well, and a dinky operations shack. But it's the thought that counts, and the Air Corps thought it would be a great place to put a gunnery school; the weather is excellent for flying and there was plenty of government land available for a dollar an acre. The land was cheap be-

cause it really wasn't much good for anything except gunnery practice. You could bomb it into oblivion and never notice the difference.

Las Vegas Army Air Field quickly grew—at one point it was turning out more than 800 B-17 gunners and copilots every five weeks. The base shut down in 1947, but reopened again in 1948 as Las Vegas Air Force Base, providing the Air Force with advanced single-

Next page
The rear office of the F/A-18D striker. The back-seat WSO can see to the distribution of a wide variety of smart and dumb munitions, regardless of weather or darkness. Joe Towers

engine pilot training. That mission changed when the United States got into the Korean War, and almost every American jet pilot that stalked MiG Alley learned his stuff over the Great Basin.

When the Air Force changed the names of its bases to honor its heroes instead of geographic areas, Las Vegas Air Force Base became Nellis AFB in 1950. Lt. William Harrell Nellis was a seventy-mission P-47 pilot from Las Vegas. Nellis was killed on 27 December 1944 over Luxembourg; he was twenty-eight years old.

Lieutenant Nellis would certainly be in awe of the base that bears his name today. It has more than 10,000 employees and a payroll approaching $200 million. Nellis AFB was the largest base in the old Tactical Air Command, and no doubt maintains that honor in the new Air Combat Command. It is a rare American fighter pilot who has never visited Nellis. The fancy new sign at the main gate says it all—"Home of the Fighter Pilot."

Red Flag is a big part of the overall picture at Nellis, but it's far from the whole story. The Fighter Weapons Center at Nellis has Red Flag under its administrative wing, along with a number of other entities: the Fighter Weapons School, Air Warrior Support to the Army's National Training Center at Fort

A Falcon lugs two live 1,000-pound Mark 84s, the better to rearrange some desert real estate. James Benson

Irwin, California; the Thunderbirds Air Demonstration Squadron; operational testing and evaluation of modern fighter weapons; fighter tactics development and evaluation; adversary/aggressor tactics research; and the Nellis Range Complex. Also under Nellis control is Indian Springs Auxiliary Air Field, an austere base on the south edge of the ranges.

Most of these functions are grouped in a traditional Air Force wing structure. The 57th Fighter Wing doesn't carry many aircraft on its books, at least not compared with a conventional fighting outfit. It does, however, conduct

a number of different operations, many of them unique in all the Air Force. Before we delve into Red Flag itself, let's take a look at Nellis' other operational divisions.

Fighter Weapons School

This is postgraduate education for the best fighter pilots in the Air Force, along with a small number of guest students from other branches of the American military and from other air forces around the world. The normal curriculum covers eight weeks, during which time the students will take in the latest gouge

The US Air Force Thunderbirds form up and call for smoke under the window of their KC-135 tanker. The team is based at Nellis AFB when not on the *show circuit. Winter practice for new members is conducted at Indian Springs Auxiliary Field north of Nellis.* George Hall

on fighter tactics, missiles, countermeasures, and the changing strategies of air warfare. The school flies its own inventory of modern tactical jets, including F-15s, F-16s, F-15Es, F-111s, and A-10s. The school jets, seen frequently in the Nellis pattern, carry the tail code WA. While they are often seen in the traffic jams related to Red Flag launches and recoveries, they almost never participate in actual Red Flag missions.

The students and instructors at the Fighter Weapons School get in plenty of flying, with emphasis on one-on-one fights, section and division tactics, and the more specific mission-related employment of dedicated aircraft like the F-15E and the A-10. But the students don't go flying as much as they'd like, and classroom hours far outweigh flight hours.

The bottom-line idea, as with the Navy's TOPGUN school, is to teach the students the most current doctrine and information on fighter and strike tactics, so that they can pass the hot poop along to their squadron-mates back home. The goal, which is almost universally realized, is to have at least one Fighter Weapons School graduate in every Air Force tactical squadron, and a TOPGUN grad in every Navy or Marine Corps tactical unit.

The Fighter Weapons School also has a hand in up-to-date test and evaluation of tactics and hardware. Nellis is an excellent site for this sort of work, since it is adjacent to one

A Shaw AFB-based F-16C gets down to 100 feet AGL on a simulated bomb run. George Hall

of the Air Force's most thoroughly instrumented ranges. Nellis shares test duties with two other Air Force bases, Edwards in the Mojave Desert and Eglin in the Florida panhandle. Each has an area of specialization: Nellis concentrates on evaluating and modernizing aerial tactics and doctrine; Edwards is more geared to the actual flying properties of new or modified aircraft; and Eglin is the place where missiles and ordnance are test-fired and exploded on instrumented targets. Navy and Marine aircraft and weapons are similarly tested at Naval Air Station (NAS) China Lake next to Edwards, NAS Point Mugu on the southern California coast, and NAS Patuxent River in southern Maryland.

The Thunderbirds

It would be tough to find a plane lover anywhere in the United States who has never watched the US Air Force Thunderbirds in action. Without question one of the world's premiere military acrobatic teams, the TBirds base out of Nellis when they're not traveling the air-show circuit. In a normal year, the team will travel 50,000 miles and put on eighty aerial displays before a total crowd of some ten million people.

Thunderbirds duty is normally a two-year tour, and it's the ultimate ticket-punch for a career-minded jet pilot. Several new pilots join the team each fall; they practice for several months in the winter, usually in the airspace

A Hog lets fly with its 30mm anti-tank cannon. The gun's reverse thrust is equal to that of a J-79 jet in afterburner, and Warthog drivers report being *hurled forward in their shoulder straps when they squeeze on the loud handle.* George Hall

39

A quick rolling check of the wheel brakes is part of the F-16's start-up checklist. Lans Stout

near Indian Springs Auxiliary Air Field (AAF) just north of Nellis. Then the show season kicks off in late spring, and the team doesn't see much of Nellis until fall rolls around again.

What sort of Air Force pilot becomes a Thunderbird? Unlike normal squadron duty, it's not an administrative assignment; the pilot has to make his wishes known to the team, and has to be approved by all the pilots. Of course he has to be a hot stick, with certain minimum levels of flying experience in tactical jets. But the Thunderbird routines, surprisingly enough, aren't really all that different from day-to-day fighter stuff—just a bit more precise and deliberate. In other words, most Air Force fighter pilots can handle the flying with the requisite amount of practice.

A Thunderbird has to be a lot more than simply a great jet pilot. He has to be personable, a good public and sound-bite speaker (you'd be surprised at how many pilots are downright nonverbal), enthusiastic about the Air Force, and able to answer the same stupid

A Mirage pilot pulls on the stick as he scoots away from a desert target. George Hall

question 300 times while acting as if he's never heard it before. And let's face it, he has to look the part: slim and trim, wavy hair, gleaming teeth, the living embodiment of the fighter pilot hero. After all, the very expensive Thunderbirds operation is first and foremost a public awareness and recruitment device, and the team members are salesmen as well as pilots.

Since I've caught myself using the pronoun "he" a number of times in the preceding paragraph, this might be a good place to interject a few words about women pilots in the Air Force. They certainly exist, although not in spectacular numbers—about 3 percent of the total in the Air Force and Navy, more like 10 percent in Army aviation, and a big goose egg in the Marine Corps. In today's Air Force, women are still restricted to flying noncombat types: tankers, transports, AWACS, and the like. Female instructors fly the T-38 advanced jet trainer, and a small number with test pilot training do get to fly fighters in evaluation programs.

But big changes are in the works. Though loath to admit it, our Air Force works for you and me, and Congress has made it clear that it's time for all military flying opportunities to be opened up to qualified women pilots. A lot of the men won't like it, but they'd best grow up and get used to it.

Women flew combat daily in the Gulf, law or no law, and several female Army helicopter types were killed in action. A woman Thunderbird in the near future? Probably, although this is a tricky prospect for the Air Force, not because of concern about a woman doing the job, but because of fear that a woman team member would lead 50,000 teenage girls to set their sights on being fighter pilots.

Back to the all-male Thunderbirds of today. They fly a jet that's not only a great tactical fighter but a great show plane as well, the F-16 Fighting Falcon. The little Electric Jet is so powerful that even pure vertical maneuvers in the TBirds routine are performed at something like 65 percent power. Obviously, pilot applicants with F-16 time will have a certain advantage in rushing the team, but that's not an absolute; the current team includes an A-10 Warthog driver, for instance. Thunderbird pilots don't merely check out in the Falcon; their jets can be repainted and rearmed (they normally fly without the internal 20mm cannon) in forty-eight hours, and the team pilots can go off to war that rapidly if need be. They'd attach to the 58th Fighter Wing out of Luke AFB, Arizona, in the event of total mobilization. The team pilots maintain

Two Navy Tomcats blow in from the west to hassle Blue strike aircraft. The F-14s have long been popular additions to Red Flag defensive forces. Tom Twomey

A co-ed crew hooks up a data pod on the underwing station of an F-111 participating in Red Flag. The unit sends a constant stream of digital data to ground receivers on the range, yielding real-time info on the jet's position, speed, attitude, and weapons availability. George Hall

the same level of basic proficiency in the F-16 that is expected of all Air Force Falcon drivers. The Navy's Blue Angels have a different take on this concept. They fly their F/A-18 Hornets only as demonstration aircraft, and they don't maintain a secondary combat capability, short of returning to their former fleet squadrons in the event of the Big One.

Air Warrior

This relatively new program involves 57th Fighter Wing pilots flying close air support (CAS) missions in connection with operations at the Army's National Training Center. The NTC conducts the Army's version of Red Flag at Fort Irwin, a desolate desert outpost some seventy-five air miles west of Nellis, in California. Army training at this Mojave Desert base over the past decade served as superb preparation for the lightning ground war in

Iraq and Kuwait. The terrain and environment are almost identical (that is to say track-less sandy desert, unbelievably bitter cold in the winter, and temperatures up around 120 degrees in the summer). This is where Patton came to train the inexperienced armor forces that ultimately joined the Brits in smashing the Afrika Corps on the fringes of the Sahara.

The Army uses the Red Flag model to train whole mechanized and armored divisions in mock war scenarios. They have their own Aggressors (had them, in fact, long before the Air Force and Navy picked up on the idea), professional enemies who do nothing but lurk around the desert waiting to attack unsuspecting Blue forces. Electronic threats and simulators are used profusely, and laser rangefinders calculate antitank shots with great accuracy. And given the Army's current AirLand Battle doctrine, there is heavy integration of Army air assets (read helicopters) at all levels of the fight.

The Air Force supports this training with A-10 and F-16 hops by 57th Fighter Wing birds flying from Nellis and Indian Springs. Forward air control versions of the Warthog, equipped with extra FM radios and designated OA-10, work with ground forward air controls (FACs) to call and mark targets for the fast-movers. (Actually it's a kindness to refer to the Warthog as a fast-mover, since it's hard-pressed to stay in front of the hottest helicopters. A favorite Hog cartoon shows a head-on view of an Iraqi tank at flank speed, with an angry A-10 close behind. The tank commander, his head sticking out of the hatch, is yelling to his driver, "Faster, Mahmoud! He's gaining on us!") The jets also practice engaging ground targets with smart laser-guided weapons, the necessary laser designation being provided by hovering helicopters or portable units in the hands of ground troops.

The F-16s flying Air Warrior missions are refining close air support tactics for the decidedly fast-moving Falcon. The quandary is as old as close air support itself: fly slow to maximize the accuracy of your weapons and you'll take ground fire; fly at the speed of heat and you won't even see the bad guys, much less hit them. The A-10 is the ultimate weapons platform for supporting troops, except for the question of survivability; if it tangles with an enemy that's serious about shooting back (unlike the hapless Iraqis) it's going to get hit and hit again.

The Air Force is determined to turn the Falcon into a successful CAS bird, although results in Kuwait were nothing to shout about. The Warthog kicked severe butt in the Gulf War, but hardly anyone was taking the trouble to shoot back; despite its superb performance against enemy ground forces, there is a strong movement within the Air Force to phase out the A-10 before it winds up in a ground war where the threats are a lot more menacing. Enter the F/A-16, the down-and-dirty attack version of the fighter with all the latest gadgets for precise day-night navigation: Navstar GPS (Global Positioning System), dual INS (Inertial Navigation System), LANTIRN (Low-Altitude Navigation and Targeting Infrared for Night), terrain following radar, and more. The Pentagon is proceeding with plans to modify up to 400 F-16Cs to this standard by the mid-1990s.

The Air Warrior Falcon pilots are working from a script written back on the other side of the country. An Air National Guard unit, the

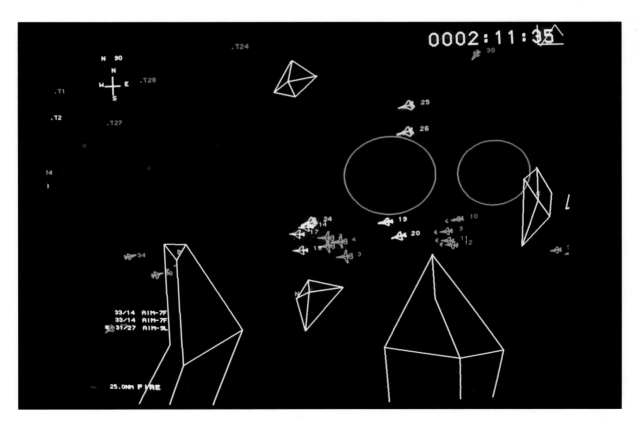

RFMDS (Red Flag Measuring and Debriefing System) provides a color digital representation of the mission in real time. Blue strikers can be seen entering the ranges through Student Gap, as Red defenders lurk at varying altitudes to the north and west. George Hall

An RFMDS operator can view the battle simultaneously from a number of different electronic vantage points—from individual cockpits to a God's-eye view of southern Nevada. George Hall

138th Fighter Squadron "Boys from Syracuse," was in the process of writing the CAS instruction book for the Falcon when the Gulf War loomed. They put that chore aside and went to war *en masse,* along with another Guard F-16 outfit from South Carolina. Once in action their missions had, in time-honored military fashion, almost nothing to do with CAS; they courageously soldiered on with several unrelated jobs, including lots of bombing and even an improvised variation of the Wild Weasel SAM-suppression mission.

Back in New York and relatively unscathed, the Boys got back to work on turning the Falcon into a low-and-fast striker. Many of the same pilots had written a similar manual for the A-10 a decade before. The task contin-

ues, with the 138th flying older F-16As (the Boys have been promised C-models) fitted with a huge centerline gun pod. It contains the GAU-5 antitank cannon, a slightly scaled down version of the Warthog's 30mm monster. Weight restrictions permit the F-16 to load only about half as much of the depleted-uranium ammunition as the Hog carries, but with a judicious trigger finger the gun is just as deadly to most armored vehicles. For various reasons the A-10 with the heavier gun still

Next page
The microwave links above BLACKJACK provide real-time contact with threat videos and date receivers on the Nellis ranges. George Hall

gets much better results; in fact, the Syracuse unit fooled around with the GAU-5 for only one day of the Gulf War before yanking them off the jets for the duration. Subsequent tests with the pod have yielded such indifferent results that the program is all but dead.

In the past several months the Air Warrior missions have focused on the terrible problem of friendly fire casualties. It's a tragic and unacceptable fact that fully one-fourth of all the coalition's combat deaths in Desert Storm were caused by its own people. The Army lost several M1 main battle tanks; every one of them was shot by another M1. It's clear that nothing can be much more important than developing procedures, techniques, and hardware to keep these mistakes from happening in another war. It's probable that friendly fire accidents can never be eliminated entirely, but all branches must strive to correct the disastrous mistakes made in the Gulf War. Perhaps the key isn't in the realm of policies and electronic gadgets, but in the more basic areas of personal responsibility and common sense. Some of the most egregious accidents involved senior commanders urging and actually ordering subordinates to engage and destroy targets even while those

The BLACKJACK control center during a Red Flag mission. Warlord occupies the console position in the center foreground. George Hall

subordinates were frantically requesting confirmation of the targets' hostile intent.

The Nellis Range

Air Force and Navy ranges and Military Operating Areas (MOAs) occupy almost a fourth of the very large state of Nevada. The Nellis Bombing and Gunnery Range spans the state from west to east just above Las Vegas and a bit south of Tonopah, where the F-117A stealth fighters have been based throughout their ultra-secret existence. In the northern part of the state the Navy operates its own bombing ranges east of Reno; these facilities are used mainly by Navy and Marine Corps jets flying out of the rapidly growing naval air base at Fallon. In between are millions of acres designated on flying charts as MOAs.

It's a little-known fact that it is entirely permissible for private aircraft to fly about in MOAs pretty much as they please. Permissible, maybe, but not a very good idea: military jets are cleared for supersonic flight between 100 feet and 50,000 feet above ground level (AGL) in the MOAs, and they're going to have a hell of a time spotting a Cessna tootling along at 110 knots. Memo to private pilots: Think twice before exercising your right to

The Air Force's newest Jolly Green Giant is the Sikorsky HH-60G PAVE HAWK, a gadget-laden variant of the Army's basic Black Hawk. The chop-per can navigate anywhere on earth in absolute zero visibility to effect rescues or insert special ground forces. Chad Slattery

pass through a western MOA. A supersonic F-111 could cut you in half and scarcely hear the thump.

Also, Red Flag isn't the only activity taking place on the Red Flag ranges and nearby MOAs. The Fighter Weapons School trains here, as do the Adversary Tactics Division cadre. Test aircraft from nearby Edwards AFB and adjoining NAS China Lake often overfly Nevada—could be anything from the B-2 stealth bomber to tiny, ground-hugging cruise missiles on long-distance survivability flights.

The range is subdivided into a number of carefully defined areas where certain things can and cannot happen. Live bombs can be dropped only on the numbered ranges (see map). Most of Red Flag's air-to-mud action takes place on the seventy-series ranges in the west, where reasonably realistic targets are scattered across the desert. Electronic threats, some remote-controlled and others operated by human-type desert rats, put up hostile emissions from all corners of the range.

Dead-center in the middle of any Red Flag war is a 600 square mile black hole, 50 miles due north of Indian Springs airfield, that has been referred to since the 1950s as Groom Lake (another hard-to-spot dry lakebed) or

Air Force PJs (Pararescue Jumpers) are as highly trained and conditioned as any soldiers in the world. A team of two to four PJs will go along on *every SAR flight to help find the aircrews, administer medical aid, and fight off the bad guys as needed.* Chad Slattery

Dreamland. Dreamland is probably the most secretive real estate in the United States; for decades it has been home to nuclear tests, ultra-black intelligence programs, and God knows what else. It is an understatement to say that overflying Dreamland is forbidden to Red Flag Players. Ten years ago, clipping the corner of the Dreamland box would net the offending aircrew a stern lecture and a day in the 110 degree desert playing lost pilot for the search-and-rescue people. They're even less humorous about it in 1993; do it today and you'll get an instant ticket home.

In our first edition of this book ten years back, we made a passing reference to the Dreamland Munchkins. We were just being cute, but did the UFO freaks ever come out of the woodwork! Seems that tales have been told for almost fifty years of a crash-landed flying saucer, complete with little deceased saucer people, that the Air Force has kept ever since in a deep-freeze somewhere in the Southwest. Could this be another of Groom Lake's secrets? I strongly doubt it, but as with any questions about Dreamland, the Air Force spokespeople will neither confirm nor deny. In

A three-man Marine Force Recon team jumps from a perfectly good Huey over the Nellis desert. The jarheads will attempt to link up with a downed aircrew and lead them to a safe helicopter LZ for extraction. George Hall

49

fact they dislike folks even mentioning the place, so let's get off the subject forthwith. And be sure to steer clear of it.

The capabilities of the range and its threats are constantly being upgraded, and the range control people have improvement plans laid out for the rest of the 1990s. The biggest change in the past decade has been the introduction of the Red Flag Measuring and Debriefing System, or RFMDS.

RFMDS covers the entire area of the Red Flag war with a grid of receiving sensors. Each Player carries a microwave data pod; the pod looks like a Sidewinder with no fins, and it mounts quickly on the same hard point. A microwave antenna protrudes from the pod's nose. Each jet sends a constant stream of information to the ground sensors; these receivers hand the data along via microwave to computerized comparators in the Range Control building next door to Red Flag Headquarters (HQ). The result is a real-time depiction of every aspect of the battle on large color screens. Every fight is also kept on tape for later dissection. RFMDS is a cosmic umpire that records every move of every Player, timed to the millisecond. Think you got him before he got you? Consult the RFMDS after the de-

The F-117A stealth fighter emerged from secrecy at a Nellis public open house in June 1990. George Hall

brief for the dispassionate, computerized proof.

Also in the Range Control facility is BLACKJACK, the electronic nerve center of the Red Flag war. Here Red and Blue Warlords control every aspect of the fight, in accordance with air tasking orders issued daily.

BLACKJACK controllers are also safety umpires for the whole exercise, and they can call "knock it off" to the whole package if something doesn't look right.

Range operation and maintenance is the heart of any Red Flag war, and it's a tough job. The area is large and inhospitable. Tem-

Through a decade of secrecy the Black Jet was based at Tonopah north of the Nellis ranges. The wing has recently moved into normal operating mode at Holloman AFB, Alamogordo, New Mexico. James Benson

All Red Flag activities emanate from Building 201 near the mile-long flight line. George Hall

peratures run in triple digits most of the year, with a spate of unbelievably cold weather thrown in every winter. Access roads are low-tech and tortuous. And day after day, several dozen strike aircraft are doing their best to vaporize your lovingly constructed targets. The Nellis range workers and threat operators are without question the unsung heroes of any Red Flag war.

Search and Rescue

Nellis' newest flying outfit is the 66th Air Rescue Squadron, which was reactivated in early 1991, some thirty-three years after being shut down at RAF Manston, England. Through HQ Air Rescue Service at McClellan AFB, California, the 66th's primary mission is worldwide combat rescue in support of tactical air forces. In today's Air Force this mission is mainly in the hands of Reserve and Air National Guard outfits; the 66th at Nellis is the

Air Force's first active-duty combat rescue unit geared for lightning-fast worldwide deployment.

Since its reactivation, the outfit has been flying several UH-60 Black Hawks borrowed from the Army. As of this writing the 66th is happily transitioning into the world's most sophisticated rescue chopper, the Sikorsky HH-60G PAVE HAWK. This is an expensive variant of the Army UH-60 slick, with increased fuel, an aerial refueling probe, a rescue hoist, flare and chaff dispensers for SAM protection, and an amazing array of navigation and comm equipment to permit zero-zero navigation in any environment.

The birds used for this mission in Southeast Asia, the HH-3 and the HH-53, were known as Jolly Green Giants, and they were a welcome sight to many an Air Force and Navy airman stuck on the ground in North Vietnam or Laos. The PAVE HAWK is a far more modern helicopter, and it's superior in every respect to its predecessors, except for room (or lack of it) in the main cabin. It's quicker, more survivable, more powerful relative to gross weight, and far better equipped in terms of electronic gadgetry. But it's still likely to be known as the Jolly Green, 1990s edition. The Nellis boys stick with the call sign JOLLY—and you can't blame them: There was a time when an aircrewman wearing a Jolly patch couldn't pay for a drink in any fighter pilot bar.

The typical crew on a rescue PAVE HAWK includes a pilot (right seat in a helicopter), copilot, flight engineer, and two pararescue jumpers, or PJs. The Air Force PJs, although little heralded, are among the most remarkable people in the entire American military. All are master jumpers, scuba divers, combat paramedics, mountain climbers, and all-weather survivalists. These animals undergo a year of training that makes Marine boot camp look like Club Med.

In addition to their worldwide combat role, the 66th Jollies are the primary rescue arm for the base and the ranges. They also provide backup rescue for civilian agencies in Las

Vegas and the Southwest; smaller Life Flight medical choppers often experience difficulty with sling rescues in the terrible heat-and-height conditions of southern Nevada, but PAVE HAWK can hover routinely at 5,000 feet AGL and 100 degrees Fahrenheit outside temperature, sling-lifting one victim after another.

The 66th is also involved in developing doctrine for combat rescues in the future. The Vietnam Jollies proved remarkably survivable, all things considered, although several were shot down during rescues and many others were driven off by intense ground fire. In the 1970s the emphasis shifted to a wholly new rescue technique, with highly trained ground-pounders—Army Special Forces, Navy SEALS (Sea-Air-Land), Marine Force Recon—working their way into the downed aircrew and escorting them back out on foot to a safe landing zone. This was expected to be the approved technique in Desert Storm, but it was abandoned in favor of the old-style snatch-and-grab since enemy resistance was minimal. The tragic upshot of this cockiness was the loss of two Army rescue helicopters in Iraq during the closing hours of the war.

Red Flag 92-4 in July 1992 included a number of desert rescue evolutions with the 66th flying the birds and Army Special Forces units providing both the Blue rescuers and the Red resistance forces. Various Red Flag pilots and back-seaters were tapped by their units to play injured ejection victims who had to be located and moved to a chopper LZ (landing zone). These were often two-day evolutions, with a night spent under the stars.

The Black Jet

Halfway from Las Vegas to Reno is the Tonopah Test Range Airfield, a top-secret base that remains closed to almost all visitors. From 1979 to recent months, Tonopah was home to the 37th Fighter Wing, the only unit in the world flying the F-117A stealth fighter. The wing has recently moved to Holloman AFB, New Mexico, replacing an F-15 wing as the principal tenant of the base.

Since its emergence into the light of public acknowledgment in 1990, the Air Force has toyed with various official names for the odd-looking machine. These days it's Nighthawk, but the people who work with it just call it the Black Jet.

Tonopah is a fair distance from Nellis, but it remains closely tied to the larger base. All through the top-secret 1980s, when the jets were being flown nightly over the Nevada ranges, members of the 37th left their families back in Las Vegas while working 5-1/2 day stints at Tonopah. Most of them made the weekly commute on a chartered 727 from Nellis. This placed a heavy strain on family life, especially since the wing members had to maintain complete secrecy about their mysterious work upstate. Now that the jet is more openly acknowledged, wing activities at Holloman are more typical of other Air Force tactical units. But the Black Jet still flies almost exclusively at night.

The Black Jet had an official coming-out party on the Nellis ramp in April 1990, with 25,000 dependents and civilians in attendance. A few months later it was taking up positions in the Middle East, awaiting the onset of the air war. The F-117A proved to be one of the most successful weapons in Desert Storm, flying hundreds of night precision-bombing sorties over downtown Baghdad without ever taking so much as a single hit. In fact, it was the only coalition aircraft to visit the enemy's capital city on a regular basis.

The Black Jet can be expected to take part in the after-dark portions of forthcoming Red Flag-Night Flag exercises. But some interesting problems crop up. After all, this bird is seriously invisible; it's not just hype. Unless it squawks Identification, Friend or Foe (IFF), or deploys its little radar reflector (used when it wants to increase its radar signature for safety reasons), it's going to be completely undetectable. That's potentially dangerous, with another seventy aircraft engaging in night attacks over the same targets. But hey, that's life with the Black Jet.

Red Flag

Nellis AFB's most famous tenant, along with the traveling Thunderbirds, is the training amalgam known as Red Flag. All aspects of the program are run from the Red Flag HQ, Building 201, and the adjacent Range Control facility. The buildings are within easy walking distance from the flight line, where almost one hundred military aircraft sizzle in the sun waiting for the games to begin.

Building 201 is a typical modern Air Force structure, low and squat, subdivided into a hundred rooms on two floors. Various elements of the Red Flag apparatus run the show from their offices upstairs. Every square inch of corridor wall space is taken up with commemorative plaques and photos left behind by the hundreds of units that have participated in past battles. There is a large auditorium for mass briefings. These big gatherings are held before every morning and afternoon go. It's a big space, with rows and rows of theater seats, but they still have to haul in Air Force blue folding chairs for the bigger meetings. The dais is flanked by dual slide screens, on which briefing information is projected in type so small that those without fighter pilot eyes are out of luck. Strangely, there is no clock. But you always have a good idea of the time during a Red Flag briefing because, every hour on

The Panavia Tornado, shown in desert camo over the Middle East, is an excellent fighter-bomber operated by England, Germany, and Italy. Saudi Arabia *also bought the jet when the US denied them access to modernized F-15Cs. Chris Allan*

the hour, a hundred Casio digital alarm calculator chronographs, worn uniformly by every fashion-conscious fighter jock, will engulf the auditorium in a wave of tiny beeps.

Each participating squadron is assigned a ready room for the duration of the exercise, to which the boys will retreat for further planning after each mass briefing. The aircrews also have locker space on the main floor for their flight gear. There is also a rather boring snack bar, good for little more than a chicken-wing pick-me-up at lunchtime. The Players usually adjourn at day's end to the several bars in the officers' club across the base, there to hoist a few light beers (young fighter pilots are disgustingly health-conscious) and play an addicting game called Crud. Supposedly invented by depraved Canadian F-5 pilots, Crud involves batting balls around a pool table, without benefit of cue sticks, while the combatants keep in constant motion around the table. Imagine a cross of foosball and musical chairs. Pardon the poor descriptive powers; it's a lot of fun. Marine pilots are diabolically good at it, for some reason.

Once upon a time, there was a made-for-television movie called *Red Flag: The Ultimate Game*. It still shows its face on the independent stations, usually late at night; watch for it. This was a highly unlikely tale in which Barry Bostwick (hot from *The Rocky Horror Picture Show*), an F-4 pilot, brings his wife to Red Flag but has to be introduced to his back-seater on the flight line before the first hop. Bostwick comes up with a "secret maneuver" to elude William Devane (yep, the *Knots Landing* star these days). Devane is an Aggressor pilot in every sense of the word; a man with the incisors of a puma, a Corvette roadster, and no discernible sense of humor. Seems these two were wingies in Vietnam, and they've hated each other ever since.

The plot soon lapses into pioneer mode, wandering off into ever stranger and more ridiculous directions. Good aerial dogfight footage, though, shot from the same Clay Lacy photo Learjet that did such a sensational job in the movie *Top Gun*. Things finally return to the death duel between Bostwick and his secret maneuver (which Phantom drivers everywhere instantly recognized as the Mark I F-4 Double-Handed Polish Heart Attack, although it looked a lot like a plain, old outside loop) and the terminally aggressive Devane in his F-5. Since it was after all written for TV, it quickly boils down to a 600mph car chase. The movie ends with Bostwick either leaving the Air Force in disgust or joining the Aggressors—we're not sure which. Devane winds up buying a farm, shall we say, north of Las Vegas. In the last scene Bostwick and the missus march into the Nellis hospital for a much-needed rest (he had been suffering from a case of the wimps).

The film was a sore spot for many years at Nellis, especially among the brass who reportedly approved the script and then performed violent separation maneuvers when they saw how Hollywood saw them. But the enlisteds staffing the operations desk had the right stuff, and for weeks after the movie aired they answered the phone with a cheerful "Red Flag, The Ultimate Game," until they were ordered to cut it out.

Walk across the street from 201 and gaze upon the mile-long flight line, a paradise for military tail-spotters when Red Flag (or the biennial Gunsmoke bombing and strafing competition) is in session. The war jumps off from this line twice a day, quite a feat since Nellis has only one pair of active runways. Usually some of the Players take on an austerity scenario and operate out of the no-frills Indian Springs auxiliary airfield some twenty miles closer to the ranges; this alleviates some of the parking problems at Nellis.

The guest fighters and strikers usually occupy the southern edge of the tarmac. Foreign visitors take the first rows, and the Navy or Marines come next. Then come the Air Force Players—F-15s, F-16s, F-111s, and A-10s. Farther north are the permanent tenants of the Fighter Weapons School and Air Warrior. The Adversary Tactics Division MiG simulators stage from here also. On up the line are the Thunderbirds, when they're off the road. And

at the north end of the field is an immense new expanse of concrete that is specially reinforced to handle the heaviest of aircraft. This is where the big guys hang out—B-1s, B-52s, and AWACS, and the transports that bring people and parts to the war. Loaf around Nellis long enough and you'll see every military bird in the current inventory.

A word about visits might be in order. It is possible to go on scheduled tours at the base; a call to the public affairs people will yield the necessary information. But Nellis, like all US air bases, is a highly secure facility. No one outside the military can enter the base without an escort, and the security police take interlopers very seriously.

And no photography on the flight line without an escort and permission from the folks who run the ramp—don't even *think* about it. A feature of all tactical US air bases is a red line painted on the concrete, separating the parked aircraft from the rest of the base. Every few hundred feet there is a break in the line; people and vehicles pass through these gaps, and *only* through these gaps. The red line simulates a high blast-proof wall, something that actually exists at some bases in Europe. No one can step over the red line, even accidentally. This may sound silly, but it's treated very seriously. Cross the red line and you are certain to find yourself face-down on the sizzling concrete, an M-16 at your neck, and a slavering Rottweiler barking in your ear. Hey, it's happened to me, and it can happen to you.

Red Flag is planned at Nellis, briefed and debriefed at Nellis, staged out of Nellis. But the real action is up north, in the spotless skies over the ranges. Time to take a closer look at the opposing forces, Red and Blue, that will soon be beating up on each other just west of Student Gap.

French Air Force Mirage 2000s fire up on the Red Flag ramp. The crew chiefs obviously have some experience in dressing for desert climates. George Hall

Chapter 3

Red Force

Welcome to Redland, a mythical country ravaged every two months or so by hypothetical wars. Geographically, Redland is located entirely within the borders of Nye County, Nevada. Politically, it is in another corner of the globe. Until recently, Redland usually was an imaginary member of the now-defunct Warsaw Pact—Commie to the core and proud of it. Nowadays it can be a little oil-oozing sandlot, a tropical hell in the Western Pacific, a famine-wracked bandit haven in East Africa, or a Haiti-like cancer in the Caribbean.

The Red Flag intelligence types insist on reminding us that Redland is completely "notional," that no inference should be drawn in comparison with any real trouble spots. Well, OK. Red Flag owns Redland and can say anything it wants. But Redland fits the bill for the Standard All-Purpose Hostile Country, a nation composed of targets and threats. This is the way the military often sees the world, and rightly so.

Redland's 1,500 square miles of worthless real estate is delightfully target-rich, and is fiercely defended by one of the most sophisticated integrated air defense systems (IADS) in

Red defenders for Red Flag 92-4, FAZER flight out of Luke AFB, Arizona, get a quick top-off from a KC-135R tanker before pitching into the fight. George Hall

the world. None of this does the Redlanders much good, though, because their country declares war on and is consistently trounced by the US Air Force and its buddies. Trounced five or six times a year, depending on budgets, in wars that always last six weeks, in campaigns that always involve exactly ten flying days. Like America, Redland is a civilized country that never fights on weekends.

Redland—or Scirroco in Red Flag Exercise 92-4—is a singularly unappealing place to live. It is bordered on the east by the peace-loving and democratic Blue nation (Cavalier this time around), whose borders extend to the Mormon Duchy of Utah. Scirroco abuts the empire of California to the west. Up north is Green Nation, always neutral in these little spats, the Switzerland of the desert. Redland/Scirroco's entire Gross National Product, it seems, is squandered on defense. It has no cities, few roads, airfields with planes that never move, and a railroad that goes from nowhere to nowhere. On Redland's national flag is a FAN SONG radar antenna. Its national anthem is the ominous growling that American aircrews hear coming from their electronic countermeasures gear.

The premier of Redland, the generalissimo of Scirroco, is none other than an American Air Force major! And he rules the country, not from a heavily defended capital or presidential palace, but from a government-issue desk in

Building 201 at Nellis Air Force Base, just down the hallway from the Red Flag commander's office! No wonder he always seems to know what the noble Blue forces are up to.

The major, of course, denies he is supreme commander of anything. He says he is merely the Red Flag intel chief, head of the little unit that creates the scenarios for realistic warfighting threats. Sure. Next he'll be claiming that Scirroco isn't in the grip of the dreaded General Naptha, who overthrew the duly constituted government in a violent coup six weeks ago. Back in the good old days of Communist enemies, we referred to that as the Big Lie Technique.

Here is the enemy situation for Red Flag 92-4. Remember that this exercise has been planned as primarily an interdiction-strike

The Marine Corps uses the AV-8B Harrier II jump-jet as its principal close air support attacker. The little jet can stage from unimproved LZs (landing zones) only a few miles from the action. This bird is carrying four Mark 82s plus a pair of Sidewinders for air defense. George Hall

scenario, with F-111s serving as the core airplanes and with lots of mid-altitude strike tactics in the forefront. It seems that General Naptha has total control over the richest country in the region; Scirroco's oil, platinum, and cobalt wealth have been translated into a state-of-the-art military machine with both Soviet-made and American equipment in profusion. The countryside is studded with the latest and deadliest Soviet SAMs and radar-aimed AAA. MiG-29 Fulcrums and Su-27 Flankers are flown by Russian-trained pilots, and a squadron of F-16s, bought from an unsuspecting America, is in the hands of unscrupulous US mercenaries. The jets operate from three heavily defended airfields.

Some 2,000 Russian advisors remain in the country; they were brought over by the Socialist government that ruled Scirroco through the 1980s, and they have no interest in returning home. A resistance movement has fled Scirroco and is operating in exile from Cavalier, including a sizeable contingent of Army and Air Force personnel. The situation is deteriorating by the day. A United Nations (UN) embargo has been partially effective, but further joint action is likely. Expect a US-led coalition to attack Scirroco in an effort to return the deposed Christian Socialist leader, Enrique Guy Degas, to his elected office.

Red Flag's adversary pilots are a bit short on real-life MiGs, although that could change one of these days, what with cash-hungry Russians reportedly peddling Fulcrums for as little as $1 million apiece. In the absence of the real thing, however, F-16C Falcons will fly the Red counter-air missions in Red Flag 92-4. The Adversary Tactics pilots based at Nellis will lead the pack with a four-ship of their distinctive camouflaged jets, accompanied on different days by Falcons from MacDill AFB, Florida, Luke AFB, Arizona (these guys are fighter lead-in instructors, who usually have to ride around in the back seat watching their students do everything wrong), and Ramstein AB, Germany (these are the jets that carry the superb new AIM-120 AMRAAM, a weapon so capable that it has to be left out of this exercise for fear of altering the balance of power too drastically).

It's not normal for the Red air defense to be so uniform. In other Red Flags, all sorts of dissimilar fighters have tried their hand at this job, including Navy F-14s (enjoined like the Ramstein crew from using their best missile, the ultra-long-range AIM-54 Phoenix), Marine Corps F/A-18s, French Mirages, and British Panavia Tornados. The best training is achieved with a mix of defenders, the weirder and harder-to-identify the better. Unfortunately the Navy and Marines are really feeling the money crunch, and they've been forced to cut back on their Red Flag involvement.

These defenders will CAP (combat air patrol) the obvious targets and attempt to break up the strikers as they roll in from the east. Of course, the attack craft won't come in alone; they will be escorted in Red Flag 92-4 by as many as twelve F-15 Eagles. The Scirrocan F-16s will find themselves engaged by the Eagles long before visual contact. They'll no doubt take Beyond Visual Range (BVR) Sparrow hits (simulated, of course) and they'll be ordered by their BLACKJACK controllers either to regenerate over a certain landmark before reentering the fight or to consider themselves killed for the day. It can be very frustrating to hear Eagle drivers calling Fox 1 shots on you when you've scarcely left the tanker, but these days it's perfectly realistic. The Eagle has a much more powerful radar than the smaller Falcon, and can lock up and take a shot before the Falcon knows anyone is out there. In the Bekaa Valley air battles, Israeli Eagles achieved Sparrow hits on Syrian MiG-21s that were just lifting from their runways and retracting the gear.

The Red jets attempt to simulate tactics that American pilots might expect to encounter in the rest of the 1990s. The Soviet threat has faded, but Russian-built jets are everywhere. And so are Russian training, tactics, and air defense hardware. Since Russian on-board radars have traditionally lagged behind Western gear, their fighter pilots (and the pilots they've trained) have relied on

ground-based radar controllers to give them target vectors by radio. These techniques are usually a part of Red Flag, with the Red aircraft using their own adversary controllers and radio links operating from a corner of the BLACKJACK control room.

The Scirrocan F-16s are going to try to call shots on some of the strikers, but it will be tough work. In the first place, the strike escorts (F-15Cs from Keflavik, Iceland, and from Tyndall and Eglin AFBs in Florida) will try to engage the enemy fighters and distract them from the strike package, just as the Mustangs and Spitfires did in World War II. Second, some of today's strike aircraft can convert in an instant to air-to-air mode, even with a load of bombs aboard. The F-15E Eagle fights like a bear, as does the British Tornado. (Smaller bombers like the air-to-mud F-16 can't really dogfight successfully without jettisoning their ordnance.) Two bomb-laden Navy Hornets heading into Iraq picked up a pair of Iraqi MiGs on the nose, dispatched both with one missile apiece and almost no maneuvering, then continued on with successful attack missions.

And there's a third point. Safety comes first at Red Flag, and one of the Rules of Engagement (ROE) calls for Red defenders to lay off any striker that is on a final bomb delivery run with live ordnance. It's not particularly realistic—in fact, that's when he's most open to rear-quarter attack—but wildly inaccurate bombing could result, and that could lead to damaged threat-generating equipment and danger to the ground operators.

Still, the attackers will find themselves contending with enemy fighters, along with everything else they have to worry about. The Adversary Tactics Division pilots and their

The EF-111A Raven is the dedicated electronic-warfare version of the F-111 Aardvark, able to accompany a supersonic strike package and provide reliable SAM jamming on the way in and out. The Raven and the Navy/Marine Prowler proved extremely dependable in Desert Storm. James Benson

The "Smoky SAM" is a low-tech but thoroughly realistic missile simulator. Newer versions can reach altitudes of 10,000 feet or more. Michael Skinner

visiting wingmen will use the building-block approach first employed by the Aggressor squadrons. They'll take it relatively easy on the Blue forces in the early engagements, getting increasingly tenacious as the two-week campaign develops. Any Blue bird can expect a bounce on any hop, be it an F-111, a B-52, or even a C-130 Hercules on a tactical resupply mission. Note that tankers and command-and-control aircraft (E-2C and E-3B AWACS, RC-135s, E-8A Joint STARS, and so on) are off-limits to defending fighters, again due to safety constraints. This is another example of realism taking a back seat, but these trade-offs are regrettably common at Red Flag. The tankers and the airborne controllers are two of the most critical elements in any modern air war, and a savvy enemy would consider them dream targets for his defending fighter assets.

The earlier Red Flags had a much larger fighter-vs.-fighter component than they have today. The Gulf air war brought into perspective the tremendous importance of attack aviation. The strikers and bombers have said it since World War II: Why zoom around the sky killing the enemy one at a time when you can kill him by the hundreds on the ground? The dramatic emergence of reliable precision-guided munitions has focused the strikers' arguments even further.

Fighter jocks will be loath to admit it, but they're going to be underemployed in any possible late-1990s air war. Iraq was by all measures a credible aerial enemy, with a large and reasonably well-trained air force made up of hundreds of current Russian and French jets. Yet, two days into the air war they had ceded their skies to the Coalition aircraft. Their airborne warning and control nets had been totally shattered, and their half-blind scrambles threw them up into an arena filled with hundreds of adrenaline-charged, fangs-out fighter pilots serious about killing. No wonder they proceeded to sneak a couple hundred planes into Iran (where they remain today, sporting new paint jobs).

There are plenty of potential enemies and hot spots on the horizon, but it's hard to point out even one that could conceivably mount a convincing air-to-air fighter defense. It's no wonder the Red Flag air campaigns are shifting so determinedly into all-out attack mode.

But an enemy hard-pressed to launch a fighter defense can still throw up a dreadful amount of black trash from the ground. And Red Flag reflects this reality. For every Blue Player that gets "shot down" in an aerial engagement, there are several that take mock hits from ground AAA and missiles. Again, the Gulf War experience showed that even a punchy, starving, and thoroughly demoralized enemy can keep on shooting at airplanes until the last moments of battle. Over the Kuwait lines, damage to our low-down attackers, primarily A-10s and Marine AV-8B Harriers, was considerable.

Red Flag planners have put an impressive amount of energy and effort into the upgrading of both targets and threats on the range. Targets are an ongoing dilemma, what with skilled attackers bombing and strafing them almost daily with live ordnance. The trick is to

A Navy EA-6B Prowler radar jammer over the tundra north of CFB Cold Lake, Alberta. The systems in the Prowler and the Air Force EF-111A Raven can defeat most known SAM radars, and the jets can also fire anti-radiation missiles to destroy ground transmitting sites. Robert Lawson

assemble targets that look real from the air while being easy and cheap to reassemble after getting repeatedly blown to pieces. Range airfields actually have derelict fighters in earthen revetments, as well as realistic runways and buildings. There are some pretty neat Scud launchers, made from telephone poles and B-52 drop tanks. And a new twist is a column of cinder-block tanks that contain heat sources to put out realistic infrared signatures. Although they sound (and are) crude, they look amazingly real when the juices are pumping and you're blowing into the target area at 500 knots.

One F-15E back-seater, with fifty-five Gulf missions and nine Red Flags under his belt, told me about an airfield attack in central Iraq. Although most Strike Eagle missions were at night, numerous delays had caused this particular mission to slip and slip until dawn. As the ground slowly lit up, the two-person crew saw their enemy for the first time with their eyes instead of via the green LANTIRN (Low-Altitude Navigation and Targeting Infrared for Night). Both pilots blurted to each other on the intercom: "It looks just like Tolicha Airfield on the range!" Quite an attaboy for the Red Flag target maintenance folks.

Where there are targets, there are going to be threats. The range folks have added steadily to their threat inventory for years, and things only get worse for the Blue forces. Some of the threats are plainly visible, like AAA pits and older Russian SAMs as big as power poles (actually they *are* power poles, painted silver with red nose cones). Others are strictly electronic in nature, designed to increase the pucker factor by "painting" the attack jets and calling for a response from the on-board countermeasures.

Actual live bombing is done only on the numbered ranges; there are real live citizens and range employees in the Military Operating Areas, so those parts of the range are out of bounds for ground attacks. And some of the numbered ranges are used mainly for test and evaluation of new equipment and tactics. This leaves the seventy-series ranges, and this is where most of the air-to-desert action takes place at Red Flag. Ranges R-71, R-74, R-75, and R-76 are studded with perhaps a hundred targets, both real and kluged: industrial areas, railheads, airfields, pipelines, and loads of vehicles, armor, SAMs, and guns.

As the Players fly east to west, the targets are arrayed so as to simulate the Forward Edge of the Battle Area (FEBA), the rear echelons, and the enemy's homeland. Vehicular targets and threats will be encountered first, in R-74. This is A-10 country when they're brought to Red Flag.

But weed-whackers will encounter radar-controlled AAA like the Russian-built ZSu-23 Zip Guns, actually some old Army M-114 scout cars fitted with little radars from Navy F-5 fighters. They combine to do a good impression of the ubiquitous four-barreled Shilka and its GUN DISH fire-control radar. Lots of third-worlders tend to switch off the radar in favor of the old point-and-shoot, and the sheer volume of 23mm rounds can make up for indifferent aiming skill. The Zip Gun has been a dreaded weapon since the early Vietnam days, and like the US-made HAWK, the damned thing is everywhere.

Farther west, in ranges R-75 and R-76, the strike package will encounter supply points and industrial targets, defended for the most part by bigger 57mm AAA and all kinds of radar-controlled SAMs. The most modern Gulf War tactics call for mid-altitude approaches over these threats with accompanying electronic jammer aircraft tasked with the neutralization of these assets. It worked for the Israelis in Lebanon's Bekaa Valley, and it worked for the Coalition over Iraq. The jamming birds—the Wild Weasels, the Navy EA-6B Prowlers, and the EF-111A Ravens—do their work so well that they've become the 1990s version of the Vietnam Jollies, the guys who can't pay for a drink in a fighter pilot bar.

The Red Flag threat operators evaluate the ability of the jammer-suppressors to frighten them into shutting down their control radars. In the Gulf the Navy Prowlers joined the Weasels in carrying High-Speed Anti-Radiation Missiles (HARMs) on their rails as well as jamming pods, the better to present the Iraqi missileers with a simple choice: turn off the radar or die.

In case one of the ground radars does manage a good lock, the desert rats will launch a Smoky SAM. This is a very low-tech simulator, but all Red Flag participants report that it really, really gets your attention. Smoky SAM is a few bucks' worth of toilet-paper roll, cardboard fins, and model rocket motor. They aren't really pointed *at* anyone, just straight up. But they leave a thousand feet worth of billowing white smoke trail, and they're said to have been a real shot in the arm for laundry businesses around Nellis.

Smoky SAM was developed at the China Lake Naval Weapons Center after Red Flag and TOPGUN pilots complained that a lockup wasn't a scary enough threat indicator. And besides, what about those shoulder-fired heat-seekers like the Russian SA-7 Grail and the American Stinger? They don't give the pilot a RHAW (Radar Homing and Warning) indication; if he doesn't see them coming and drop flares, he's going to take a hit. In the works is a more sophisticated Smoky that can actually guide and turn a little bit.

Any honest pilot who's had the experience will tell you that there's nothing so terrifying as the reality of an enemy SAM guiding on little old you. An F-16 squadron commander from Shaw AFB in South Carolina tells a story

Many ground threats are slaved to television systems that show the aircraft in all their vulnerability.

All flights are taped for later viewing by the aircrews. It's not always a pretty picture. George Hall

67

about evading a big SA-3 over Iraq, as the Guard channel squealed with warnings from wingmen. His every jink was matched by the Mach 3 missile. Finally a violent max g-force yank at the last nanosecond threw the missile off. When he landed he could scarcely walk: he'd strained his knees and thigh muscles trying involuntarily to lift his butt away from the seat pan (against 9g loads) as the missile closed from below.

Although there is a very impressive museum at Nellis filled with the most diabolical air-defense machines from all countries (only open, unfortunately, to those with the proper security clearances), the Air Force insists that there is no Russian-made or other foreign gadgetry out on the Nellis ranges. Various American radars have been tweaked and modified to reproduce the frequencies, pulse widths, and scan patterns associated with the most-feared enemy weapons. The ground gear usually doesn't give much of a visual cue, but the important thing is what the pilot or back-seater sees on his RHAW gear.

Besides, the pilots never see the actual radar emitters while over the targets, and thereby hangs a tale. Even though the threat operators paint big red stars on their control vans, the radar equipment is always tucked safely away in EC West and East, Pahute Mesa, and Tolicha Peak EW. Even the Zip Gun emitters have to stay five miles from any live ordnance area. This is understandable, but it's confusing for the pilots. Weasel and Prowler pilots routinely develop Red Flag Schizophrenia when they can clearly see the simulated target under their port wing, but the emissions from that simulated target are coming from a place ten miles to starboard. This is especially frustrating when they are tasked to "destroy" the site with an antiradiation missile, since there are no emissions wafting out from the target.

Enter the Nitnoi, the remote-controlled, omnidirectional threat emitter. *Nitnoi* is a word of Vietnamese origin, meaning "no big thing." In this case, nitnois are radar transmitters mounted in hardened cases under the target. Nothing but the most direct of hits will destroy them, although their antennas, sticking out from the targets, have a very short life expectancy. But they can be replaced quickly and cheaply. These little gadgets are scattered all over the range, and pilots agree that the threat transmissions are a lot more realistic when they actually originate at the target.

Soon as many as forty of the manned sites will have television systems trained on the targets and the ingress-egress routes. These TV signals are remoted back via microwave in real time to a room in Red Flag headquarters that is filled with Trinitrons and rack-mounted VCRs. Every flight past the camera is recorded, and the tapes are edited for viewing anytime after the hop. In addition, the tape evaluators usually make up a composite tape for each unit participating in Red Flag. The tape contains the high and low points of the outfit's missions in the mock war, and the pilots can pore over it when they get home.

The tapes show not only each aircraft in living color, jinking and flare-popping like crazy if it knows how the game is played, but also a sine wave below that indicates how successful the acquisition radars are at locking up the victim for a AAA or missile shot. A strong vertical spike below the jet shows a solid lock; a wobbling straight line means no joy (failure to lock on), usually due to countermeasure signals being put out by the airplane.

I watched a day's worth of these tapes, and the viewing was highly instructive. First came an RF-4 recon Phantom at the speed of thought—low and level, but long gone before anyone could think about locking it up. Next a French Mirage 2000 did a bomb run; the pilot was throwing the handsome jet around like crazy, but for some reason he wasn't emitting anything from his normally capable ECM set. The result was a scary spike for three seconds, a long time in SAM land. Then a huge B-52, motoring along calmly at 300 knots and 300 feet AGL. No tricky maneuvers, no chaff or flares visible—but look at that perfectly flat sine wave! Lt. Col. Murky Waters interpreted: "The B-52 is old, but it has an awesome ECM setup—better in some ways than what the B-1 carries. Look at the wiggle in the line; he's jamming the bejesus out of us. You could take pot-shots at him with your AK-47, but you're not going to get him with a radar missile. No way. They do a hot job with that big puppy."

The ranges have come a long way since the first days of Red Flag, and improvements continue apace. New threats are being added to simulate the newer Russian "teen" missiles, like the SA-10 Grumble and the formidable SA-12 Gladiator.

The Iraqis showed us some heavy AAA that could have been devastating if we had left their fire-control radar systems intact. Particularly distressing was a high-rate 57mm job known to Coalition pilots as the "red rope," so called because that's what its all-tracer stream looked like. Films of Baghdad under night attack showed several of these bad boys in action.

The whole collection of threats and targets will be integrated by 1996 into a new system called JACTS, for Joint Air Combat Crew Training System. JACTS will mean range business as usual, just bigger and better in every way: more targets, some of them mobile and IR-emitting; up to 150 threats, all data-linked to BLACKJACK; twice as much TV coverage around the targets; and electronic no-drop bomb scoring that obviates the need for loading and expending real (and expensive) ordnance.

Just give a passing thought now and then to General Naptha's brave ground-pounders, the civilians (employed by defense giant Loral) who work the threats and maintain the poor targets. These people commute from Tonopah a total of four or more hours per day, most of that in four-wheel drive over nonexistent roads. They endure unbelievable weather ex-

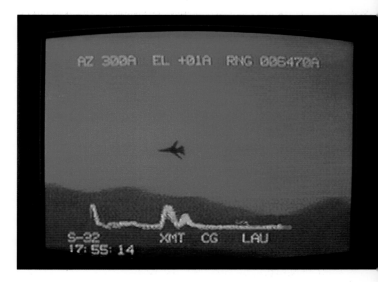

The threat video shows a low-and-fast F-111 being had by a SAM radar. The spike below the jet signals a probably fatal two-second lockup. George Hall

tremes: only a grunt who did the full Gulf tour can appreciate how incredibly cold it can get in a desert that sports 120 degree readings in July. Their day is a mix of boredom and high excitement. If a Red Flag crew seems to be in too deep, they'll cut the boys some slack. When another guy comes along who's too shit-hot for his own good, they'll bring him down to earth. They aren't exactly liked by the Red Flag Players, but they're certainly respected. They are very good at what they do.

Enough about the tyrannical Scirroco and its plans for world conquest. Let's take a look at the battle plans of the Blue forces. How do doughty Cavalier and the US-led Coalition plan to restore democracy and Just Plain Goodness to the troubled region?

Chapter 4

Blue Force

Doughty Cavalier, indeed. As conditions deteriorate toward the inevitable air war, we should take a closer look at the country we have promised to help. Cavalier is a small country that shares Scirroco's eastern border. It has a long history as a democratic monarchy with multiple parties and an elected parliament. The beloved Queen Shar'Pei has been on the throne (in power, that is) for six years. The daughter of a renowned plastic surgeon, she was sucked into marriage by the late King Lipo (pay attention, now; Intel deputy Capt. Heidi Kasel poured her little heart into this scenario) in 1974, and she has ruled benevolently ever since.

Cavalier has no real natural resources. It is predominantly a tourist mecca, especially for the elderly, because of its arid climate and the many clinics and spas centered around its glittering capital, Las Vegas. People come from far and wide to partake of the restorative waters. Unfortunately this is a flawed notion,

A two-ship of Navy Prowlers pulling on the pole over NAS Fallon to the north of Nellis. The Prowler is a stretched version of the A-6 Intruder, with a pilot plus three electronic warfare wizards to handle the large collection of jamming devices aboard. Mid-altitude strikes would be suicidal without the jamming trickery of the Prowlers and EF-111A Ravens.
Robert Lawson

as there are no waters, restorative or otherwise. We are reminded of Rick in *Casablanca*, who admitted to being misinformed in a similar situation.

But I digress. Cavalier has a minimal defense capability; in a one-to-one battle with its hostile neighbor Scirroco, it will be hopelessly mismatched. It has always had strong Western ties, and it is a member of the United Nations. Cavalier fears the worst from Scirocco, and has reluctantly agreed to allow US and Coalition forces to operate out of its huge new airport complex north of Las Vegas. Active American Air Force units will be joined in Las Vegas by the Air Force Reserve, the Air National Guard, the Canadian Armed Forces, the French Armee de L'Air, and the Fuerza Aerea de Venezuela. Marine Corps antiaircraft batteries and Army Special Forces units trained in aircrew search and rescue have also signed on. In all, twenty-two military groups or wings will be taking part.

The Blue forces are faced with complex intelligence, administrative, and planning challenges as well as the air war itself. The Red Flag planners feed information several times a day to the Blue planning staff and their intelligence people, who are drawn mainly from the core unit (in this case, the F-111 folks from Cannon AFB, New Mexico). Red Flag intel will direct strong suggestions to Blue headquarters: destroy Kawich airfield in tomorrow morning's go, or take on a new armored breakthrough this afternoon. The staff will then decide how best to solve the problem, and which unit is best equipped to handle the particular mission.

Several months before each Red Flag, a meeting is held at Nellis between the Red Flag planners and the project officers of all the units that will be taking part. At this meeting the squadron representatives attempt to fit their own desired objectives into those of the planned war. One unit might want a lot of practice with precision-guided munitions and laser designation; another may want to work on close air support; still another may be hoping for long-range intercepts with Sparrow or AMRAAM solutions.

The Red Flag folks try to give the Players what they want to the greatest extent possible. This is, after all, a training exercise and not a real war; Red Flag exists to help flying outfits work on problem areas and practice skills that may be somewhat rusty. But war is full of surprises and improvisations. Sometimes, just to keep everyone paying attention, a squadron will be tasked with a mission not on any of their want lists. Desert Storm was full of such unpleasant surprises, and there can be considerable training value in confronting the occasional unexpected problem.

An F-15E Strike Eagle takes on a load of live cluster munitions. James Benson

So war comes again to Redland and everyone chooses sides. The Blue Players join the Air Force Forces (AFFOR), the good guys. The adversaries enlist in the opposition forces (OPFOR), a term borrowed from the Army's long mock-war experience.

And the premier of Redland, the staff officer who thought the whole war up in the first place, sits back and plays the two sides against one another: "We could tell AFFOR everything that's going to happen, but we don't. We try to lead them to logical conclusions, but we certainly don't give them all the information they need. One lesson of war is that you never have perfect intelligence—never. So they have to do some very basic analysis."

And that's the way the Red Flag CO wants it: "The intelligence people are working with my ops people as if it were a war, because we also bring a lot of young TDY [temporary duty] intel people out here who have to start thinking about how you go about targeting, damage assessment, photographic intel or recon. So they look at that flow and make the targeting decisions based on the scenario that we've set up."

There's usually an aerial reconnaissance unit at every Red Flag. The intelligence personnel use the information they bring back,

The Air National Guard is about to give up the last of its beloved A-7 Corsair attack jets. This beautifully-maintained bird from Toledo, Ohio, is taking on LOX (liquid oxygen) between Red Flag missions. George Hall

73

along with other bits and pieces gleaned from debriefs of pilots immediately after they return from their missions, to work up the next day's target list. But although they decide what should be hit (along with some prompting from the Red Flag intel staffers), they don't try to tell the pilots how to hit it. That's the Warlord's job.

The Warlord is a position unique to Red Flag. Unfortunately, that exotic monicker has fallen out of favor in the past few years; he's now known less dramatically as the planning staff commander. He is in charge of coordinating all the Blue forces into a cohesive air force

that can hit the targets identified in the daily Air Tasking Orders. The Blue leader will usually be an O-5 or O-6 (lieutenant colonel or full "bird" colonel) from the core squadron. It's not necessary for him to know all the details of how each Blue unit goes about its mission. But it *is* important that the Warlord be diplomatic, and, if it comes down to it, stubborn. Otherwise some Blue units, in their natural desire to set up their missions in the most favorable conditions, might put other Blue units at a dangerous disadvantage. There's a lot of horse-trading, often at high volume, when the Warlord conducts a meeting with the different

The stubby Corsair, though subsonic and not very maneuverable, was the world's most accurate bomber until the advent of much more modern jets *like the F-15E. It has the added advantage of amazing fuel economy and resultant long "legs."* George Hall

mission commanders to put the day's strike together.

"It's that exchange between the various weapons systems operators that we're looking for," says the Red Flag CO. "If you're an F-111 pilot, you can fly for many years, and if you've never had the opportunity to sit and talk and plan a mission with Wild Weasels and jammers, with CAP, with strikers going on underneath you or close air support out in front of you—if you've never had to talk to those guys about how they go about their business—you don't have a good understanding of what they do. And that lack of understanding is going to be a severe detriment if you go to war."

This is the most exciting thing about Red Flag: getting a firsthand look at the capabilities of airplanes other than your own. The strike package is far stronger than the sum of its parts. Individual pilots tend to think that winning the war is up to them alone. But Red Flag teaches the importance of doing your thing—doing it perfectly—and letting the other guys do their stuff. If you're striking, let CAP handle the Red fighters. If you're operating at mid-altitude to escape the AAA, count on the jammers and the Weasels to negate the missile threat up there.

The actual plan to carry out the targeting assignments takes the form of "mission pack-

Warthogs out of since-closed Myrtle Beach AFB, South Carolina, start up during Red Flag 88-3. The A-10 can only participate in Red Flags that are built *around low-level attack or close air support, since the jet has no other function.* George Hall

ages." A package is a composite strike force, typically consisting of, in order: 1) photo reconnaisance flights; 2) Wild Weasels and other jammers along with fighter escorts; 3) the strikers and their fighter cover; 4) heavy strike bombers; and 5) further recon passes. Everyone will be supported by tankers, AWACS, and other electronic warfare platforms, tactical airlift and resupply, and search and rescue (SAR) forces.

"A package is a composite thought," says the Red Flag boss. "Each unit has a specific purpose and a specific tasking within the overall mission. They'll be given a specific target or job, and the threats briefed on that target—what they're supposed to do to it, and how it is defended."

The aircraft are assigned a mission code, a three-letter acronym that represents their assignment in the mission package. The mission code is mainly for the convenience of exercise planners and the range officers controlling the battle from BLACKJACK, where the numbers and lines representing the various flights are color-coded as to mission. Here are the most common Red Flag mission codes:

REC (Reconnaissance)—Flown these days by Air National Guard RF-4Cs, or by Navy or Marine jets carrying centerline tactical reconnaissance pods (TARPS). Recon can refer to visible-spectrum photography, infrared imaging, or digital information transmitted to the ground in real time.

DSP (Defensive Suppression)—This means keeping the enemy SAMs and radar-directed guns too busy or terrified to bother the rest of the package. DSP is the job of the Wild Weasels. Since the end of the Vietnam War (and all through Desert Storm) the preferred platform has been the F-4G, although F-105s and F-100s took a crack at it in the early days.

Marine Cobra gunships, along with Army AH-64 Apaches, have taken part in several Red Flags with close air support scenarios. This AH-1W model is carrying both TOW anti-tank missiles and an AIM-9 Sidewinder for air-to-air protection.
George Hall

Air Force FAC (Forward Air Controller) directs air strikes from a vantage point among the ground pounders. Small UHF radio set permits solid communications with the strikers above. George Hall

The active Air Force is trying to decide on a platform that will carry on this mission; look for either G-model F-16s or dedicated F-15E Strike Eagles to take over. One Air National Guard outfit, a former recon group (the 124th) at Boise, Idaho, will continue to deploy the F-4G for another few years. And the Air Force's few remaining Phantom Weasels are now basing out of Nellis for the time being.

OCA (Offensive Counter-Air)—This is usually airfield attack or harassment; it can be flown by fighters or light attack jets. The Guard still flies the mild-mannered but quite capable A-7 Corsair, a stubby little striker that was the most accurate bomber in the world before the F-16 came along. When the A-7s come to Red Flag (the Guard will fly them at least until 1994), OCA is the job they draw. In "our" Red Flag, 92-4, the OCA mission was handled by F-15C Eagles. In October 1992, for Red Flag 93-1, the job will be in the capable hands of the British Tornado drivers—perhaps the world's preeminent airfield despoilers.

CAS (Close Air Support)—This is the job the A-10 was built for, specifically to bomb troop positions and shoot up armored vehicles with its huge GAU-8A 30mm cannon. Army and Marine Corps attack helicopters—the Apaches and Cobras—have also flown CAS at

Red Flag, and they did plenty of it in the Gulf War as well. The Marines also use the AV-8B Harrier primarily as a CAS bird. The A-10s and the gunships sometimes operate from Bicycle Lake on the Army's nearby Fort Irwin complex. Only the occasional Red Flag features a CAS component.

BAI (Battlefield Air Interdiction)—Another favorite Warthog and Harrier mission. BAI is similar to CAS, but it is concerned with the second and third echelons behind the enemy's front lines.

FAC (Forward Air Control)—FAC is concerned with coordinating and targeting airstrikes and artillery fire. The Air Force handles the FAC mission in two ways: from the air and on the ground. A long line of unfortunate aircraft have taken on this dangerous job—single-engine Piper Cubs, push-pull Cessna O-2 "mix-masters," and most recently the tough but underpowered OV-10 Bronco twin turboprop. These days a version of the A-10, dubbed OA-10 and loaded with a few extra FM radios, is working out pretty well. In high-threat situations the FAC will probably be an Air Force pilot on the ground with the Army maneuver elements, driving a Hummer loaded with comm gear or maybe humping it with a forty-pound UHF pack radio. Red Flags often include both flying and ground-pounding FAC assets.

INT (Interdiction)—It used to be called penetration bombing. INT means striking deep into enemy territory, going for high-value targets behind the battlefield—storage points, factories, marshaling yards. This is the most complex and the most typical mission package in the Red Flags of the 1990s. The strikers can be Air Force F-111s, F-15Es, F-16s, and big guys like the B-52 and B-1B. The package can also include Navy and Marine F/A-18s, Navy A-6Es, Mirage 2000s, Panavia Tornados, and perhaps even the F-14 Tomcat. (The Navy has been doing a lot of practice bombing with the Bombcat in an effort to brighten its future as a weapons system. The jet has always been equipped with a good bombing computer, but no one ever put it to use.)

CAP (Combat Air Patrol)—This is the fighter pilot's favorite pastime, searching out and destroying enemy aircraft in dogfights. "CAP" often follows a prefix denoting the type of combat air patrol to be flown. Falcons might fly a LOWCAP at low altitude, for example, and Navy fighters protecting a carrier task force could fly a BARCAP, positioning themselves as a barrier between the ships and any bandits looking to launch antiship missiles. CAPs at Red Flag are usually the province of the single-seat F-15 Eagles. They are usually assigned different areas to CAP at different times, and sometimes they do it that way. "On a blackboard a CAP is perfectly round, and we're using our radar to search in all directions," says an Eagle driver. "Well, that's a bunch of BS—that's what we use on the blackboard. In reality you just roam the area at high speed, looking for anything you can find."

ESA (Escort)—This is the fighter pilot's least favorite form of CAP. They don't like to be too closely tied to the strike flight, preferring to pounce on the enemy from a high, hidden perch. ESA aircraft don't have to be fighters; Weasels and the EF-111A Spark 'Varks can also fly escort missions.

DCA (Defensive Counter-Air)—Formerly ADF, for Air Defense Forces. This is the bad guys' version of CAP—adversary fighter operations flown by the Red Flag staff aggressors and the other fighters tasked to help them out.

AAR (Air-to-Air Refueling)—Tanker operations, flown in racetrack ovals to the east and west of the fights. Some jets tank once and even twice on each Red Flag go; others, notably the Guard's long-legged A-7s, can fly and fight for more than three hours without reaching bingo fuel.

AWC (Airborne Warning and Control)—Radar coverage and combat air control is supplied by both ground facilities and by an E-3 Sentry AWACS bird out of Tinker AFB, Oklahoma. The AWACS orbits some distance from the fight at altitudes above 40,000 feet. It's almost always off-limits as a target at Red Flag, even though it would be Objectivo Numero Uno in any real air war. Every now and then the Red Flag planners will simulate its destruction and knock it off the air, the better to confuse the hell out of the Blue packages.

SAR (Search and Rescue)—Most Red Flags have a SAR component, especially since the base now has its own state-of-the-art combat SAR squadron. The 66th crews fly the new HH-60 PAVE HAWK, and they love to practice penetrations and extractions. Several other aircraft may be lumped under the SAR designation at Red Flag. Army Special Forces or Navy SEALs may be air-dropped from C-130s or CH-53 Super Stallion helicopters to practice locating the downed aircrew, treat simulated injuries, and assist in the extraction. And the chopper might be escorted by a couple of A-10s that will do their best to neutralize any ground fire near the LZ. This is the much-heralded SANDY mission of Southeast Asia fame, flown in those days by prop-driven A-1 Skyraiders, or Spads. It's a proven concept, and it worked great in several extractions from Iraq. Traditionalists will be glad to know that the honored JOLLY and SANDY call signs are still used.

TRS (Tactical Resupply)—This is battlefield logistics support and parachute insertion by C-130s and, in the near future, C-17s (providing, of course, they ever solve that little problem of the wings falling off when you gas it up). These missions were added to Red Flag in the early 1980s in an underlining of the Air Mobility Command's (then called the Military Airlift Command) effort to maintain a war-ready posture. From the beginning the transports were involved in Red Flag deployments, and they lobbied long and loud for a piece of the tactical action. The Hercules people are now a part of practically every Red Flag war, and they like it.

These missions help dispel the image of the transport drivers as "trash haulers"—flying civil servants with the omnipresent plastic

A two-ship of Marine Corps Hornets, each with a loadout of eight Mark 82s and two air-defense Sidewinders. George Hall

spoon in their flight suit shoulder pocket for stirring coffee during leisurely cross-country jaunts. Low-level tactical resupply missions are nasty, brutish, and long. Between legs the Herk pilots have to fly violent evasive maneuvers to throw off Red fighters, and they make sickening forty-five-degree descents into dirt strips while simulating antimissile flares and chaff. American and Canadian C-130 crews are, at this writing, playing these games for real several times a week on the perilous approach to Sarajevo. On the way in, they cross directly over the wreckage of an Italian CASA twin-prop that was shot out of the sky by a Serbian missile. Red Flag can suddenly seem a bit tame by comparison.

These are the most common Blue Players, but at one time or another practically every flying machine in the US inventory has put in an appearance. Green Flags, with their in-

An Air National Guard KC-135E tanks a Red Force F-14 Tomcat over Fort Irwin. The KC-135 must be configured on the ground for the hose-and-drogue refueling system used by Navy and Marine Corps aircraft. The newer KC-10 Extender can switch between refueling boom and hose reel while in flight.
Tom Twomey

creased emphasis on reconnaissance, electronic warfare, and intelligence gathering, bring in an odd assortment of "porcupines" (lots of weird antennas): oddly bulging C-135s, Army OV-1 Mohawks, Navy EA-6B Prowler radar jammers, even the recently retired SR-71 Blackbird. The new E-8 Joint STARS battlefield surveillance aircraft has been invited, but there are only two in existence and both are still being tested. In fact, the two big jets were pulled from their early test flights and thrust into the Gulf War on the assumption that even if they didn't work worth a nickel, they'd be better than nothing. The systems performed as perfectly as any weapon in the war. Joint STARS has a big future.

Red Flag began life as an all-Air Force ball game, but it soon occurred to the planners that bringing in outside players would be good training as well as a lot of fun. At first the Navy and Marines were brought in, usually on the Red side; then Army helicopters were invited to help out with CAS. The Canadians were obvious players, especially after they went out and bought a few squadrons' worth of F/A-18 Hornets (to them it's the CF-18). Soon the British and French were tanking over from the Old World. The Venezuelans jumped into Red Flag 92-4 with their F-16s, and the Italians sent a bunch of Desert Storm vets in their Tornados for exercise 93-1.

It is this sophisticated mix-and-match that is probably the best single thing about Red Flag training. The Desert Storm coalition is undoubtedly the prototype for practically any war scenario that can be imagined in the next two decades. The United States is not likely to engage in any serious military adventurism without allies. Our forces need to learn as much as they can about how our friends operate. Many of them—like the Brits and French, among others—are extremely good; ditto their equipment and doctrine. We have a great deal to teach one another, and Red Flag is a valuable mechanism for learning, an ideal international classroom.

Red Flag, in fact, was a harbinger of the kind of international coordination and cooper-

A Grumman E-2C Hawkeye is the Navy's carrier-based AWACS platform. They are occasionally in- *vited to Red Flag, where they usually provide airborne control of the Red Forces. Robert Lawson*

ation that made Desert Storm possible. Gen. Chuck Horner, the man who conceived and executed the allied air war in the Persian Gulf, said it in a nutshell: "Thanks to Red Flag, I had been fighting Desert Storm for ten years."

Horner tells another revealing story: "Around 1982, I was a brigadier general at Holloman. Big combined exercise in the southwest United States, with lots of participants. I get tapped as commander of all the flying assets in this whole thing, with no notice. I've got Marine reservists, National Guard, some instructors from Luke, active-duty guys—a complete patchwork. These guys show up on a weekend at Nellis, and I fly up to meet with everybody. We're supposed to fly our first missions on Monday morning! This could turn into a nightmare.

"But guess what: every one of these guys has been to Red Flag. It was amazing. It just fell into place—guys were saying, 'I'll take the so-and-so hop Monday, you take it Tuesday, air-to-air will be here, strike freq is such-and-such, you and you throw up a BARCAP here, bing, bang, boom.' They'd all done this before, and they all talked the same language. It just fell into place. The ability of people to fit into a large-scale operation, to integrate their assets with very little coordination, that's the greatest value of Red Flag training."

Horner concludes: "We need to continue pulling in as many allies as possible for Red Flag flying. Lots of the Desert Storm guys had been at least once—all of the Canadians, most of the French and Brits. It was a tremendous help."

An Air Force C-130 Hercules starts its takeoff roll at Nellis. Herks fly rough-and-tumble tactical resupply *missions in support of most Red Flag exercises.*
George Hall

Chapter 5

Edge of the Envelope

For cheerful invincibility, for maximum martial correctness, for sheer Samurai presence, it's hard to beat a modern military pilot in full combat drag. He radiates confidence and competence, filling whatever space he inhabits with the gentle rustling of the modern technological warrior. The jangling and jostling of the jacks, hoses, cables, harnesses, curraises, and Koch fittings that plug him into his jet *(and it to him!)* tinkle out a lullaby that sings, "Sleep tight, America, Daddy's got the CAP."

If you ask him he will tell you (after a nanosecond's worth of modesty, a quality that only *bad* fighter pilots are good at anyway): Hell, yes, he's the best there is, a real air-to-air Dillinger, and everybody else had better keep out of his sky. The Air Force and Navy like this attitude—they train for it, in fact—because anyone with the merest doubt in his ability has no business strapping on of their $30 million, titanium-and-silicon jets in the first place.

But the truth is, our young pilot doesn't really know how good he is. Nobody does, not even the Pentagon brass, who would certainly like to be able to pick out the aces-of-the-

A Hornet "vapes" as he yanks himself away from the Nellis targets. Such dramatic condensation displays are common in humid climates but rare around Nellis. George Hall

bases, the real killers-of-the-sky, from the Dilberts and the Whiskey Deltas before the difference becomes important. The new guy may be bright and brave, a good stick-and-rudder man with the greatest pair of hands since Luke Skywalker. But that doesn't mean he's a good combat pilot, that he'll be able to hack the mission, or even survive his first flight.

Right after the Vietnam War, *Time* magazine did a story on a Marine fighter squadron and came up with what may sound like an odd quote: "The common denominator of the guys here is that we all love to fly," said a Marine fighter type. "But the sad truth is, in terms of quantity and quality, you do your best flying in wartime."

This doesn't mean fighter jocks pray for war. But that Marine A-4 driver had the guts to say what everyone in the fighter community has known all along: there is nothing like actual combat to train fighter pilots. People say aces are born and not made; well, maybe. But you can make survivors. You make survivors the same way you make diamonds—pressure, and lots of it.

General Sherman had it right: war is hell. It is the most counterproductive activity human beings can engage in. Nobody knows the horrors of war more than the professionals our society hires to do its fighting for it. To them, there's only one thing worse than going to war, and that's going to war unprepared.

Strange things happen in wartime. People and machines are shoved to the edge with no room for error. Combat always increases the number of aircraft accidents: planes running into one another; planes hitting the ground trying to evade radar coverage; planes departing controlled flight in desperate and dangerous maneuvers. These crashes are usually not considered combat losses, but that's exactly what they are—industrial accidents inherent in the war business, the result of fear, aggression, the killer instinct, the survival instinct. Whatever you call it, it's the quality that will forever separate peacetime training from the real thing.

Aircraft are said to have an "envelope," the limits of their performance in terms of speed, altitude, g-loads, and angle of attack. The safest area is at the heart of the envelope, where there is room for error. But in order to survive and be effective, pilots must fly their aircraft to the edge of the envelope, go just a little faster or slower or higher or lower than the other guy. It's dangerous territory, hanging ten over the front edge of the board, but it's where the winners live.

Pilots have an envelope, too. There are limits to their abilities. Pilots need to know when they are flying on the edge of their personal envelope, and the trouble with most peacetime training is that they are not allowed to find out. This is understandable; training is a trade-off. There's no use in killing off pilots just to isolate the areas where they

A Holloman Eagle driver trades his bone dome for a straw cowboy hat as he deplanes after arriving from New Mexico. Temps on the Nellis concrete can reach 120 degrees F. George Hall

need more training. But the objection pilots have traditionally had about air-combat training is that in wartime they are going to be pushed to the edges of their particular envelope. And they'd prefer to find out just where that is without someone shooting at them.

American air-to-air training in the early stages of the Vietnam War was inadequate, for just this reason. The pilots were all well-trained aviators, but their preparation as warriors was not up to the demands of modern air combat. The Red Baron study and the Navy's Ault Report cited the need for more realistic air warfare training, but this was not news to most Air Force pilots. Gen. Chuck Horner says when he first went to war over North Vietnam in his F-105, he had had only a smattering of bootleg air-combat training, carried out among squadrons without the knowledge or approval of the wing. He later took part in planning the Red Flag program.

What the Red Baron study did was send a signal to Air Force and Navy brass that the trade-off between safety and realistic training was out of balance, that the lives saved through coddling training programs were not equal to the lives lost through inadequate preparation for war. It was a hard decision, a real life-and-death decision, but the Air Force decided to embark on a realistic air-combat-training regimen.

The planners realized it was going to be a dangerous proposition, especially at first. Dissimilar air combat training (DACT)—where aircraft of different types go at it under conditions as close to actual combat as possible—was, up to that time, very restricted or nonexistent precisely because it was considered so dangerous. Until safe rules for DACT could be worked out, until the majority of Air Force pilots got used to the idea, accidents were bound to happen. But the Air Force figured the accident rate would come down over time.

As it turns out, that's exactly what happened. The original rules, worked out for the Aggressor squadrons and the Navy's TOP-GUN program, were adapted for Red Flag and expanded.

The first Red Flags were truly red. There were even some murmurs of canceling the program if the accident rate didn't drop. (TOP-GUN had gone through the same thing several years before.) In all, forty-nine aircrew members have died and fifty-two aircraft have been destroyed at Red Flag since its introduction in 1975. Most of these accidents took place in the early years of the program. Pilots say that although the first Red Flags may not have been more realistic, they were certainly more sporting. But as the program has matured the accident rate has declined, even though there are now more aircraft and more missions in each Red Flag than ever before. In fact, there have been no Class A mishaps or aircrew injuries at Red Flag since the loss of an F-111F in early 1989.

"I tell the pilots just about every day that their first-priority threat out here has two subcategories and it'll kill them both times: hitting another jet and hitting the ground," says a former Red Flag CO. "Now that's number one priority for everything they do out here, recognizing that the biggest threat in this Redland territory is the ground or a midair. And if they ever get priority number two or three or four confused with number one, they'll probably get sent home in a bag. I keep telling them that this is still *simulated* war, and there is nothing at Nellis worth dying for."

Red Flag is always going to be dangerous, by its very nature. But Air Force planners have learned from experience and have formulated a set of rules that attempts to balance realism and safety. There are some pilots who complain that the rules are too wimpy, that things at Red Flag are just too far from real wartime conditions. The Brits and Israelis are famous for voicing these gripes when they visit Nellis.

But in any safety-vs.-realism issue, the American planners will always come down on the side of safety. Still, these DACT guidelines (called Rules of Engagement, or ROE) are far more realistic than the pre-Vietnam "flagpole missions," and every pilot welcomes the changes.

This list has been garnered from different sources and is meant only to represent a typical Red Flag ROE. Some units, branches of the service, and foreign forces make slight changes. The comments following each rule concern the rationale behind it and its relationship to actual combat.

1. Insure:

A. All pilots will not be scheduled for sorties or maneuvers beyond their abilities.

Each squadron's "ops shop," the office responsible for scheduling and planning missions, monitors the proficiency of each pilot to make sure he is getting enough of the right kind of training to keep "mission-ready" (MR). The wing's Standards and Evaluation (Stan-Eval) pilots give the squadron jocks check-rides, both in the sky and in simulators, to make certain the pilot and his training are up to snuff.

In terms of Red Flag, this means it's important that the pilots are authorized to fly the type of missions they will be ordered to fly over the Nellis ranges. Remember that units attending Red Flag are invited as much as a year in advance, and they're given lots of information about the type of war they're expected to fight. So it's up to the unit to get everyone prepped well before leaving for Vegas. Red Flag is no place for check-rides and cram courses. Pilots who are not mission-ready might as well stay home.

For example, during the first week of the two-week Red Flag campaign, no pilot is allowed to fly below 300 feet AGL on the ranges. In the second week, however, the jocks are permitted to fly as low as 100 feet AGL, provided their commanding officer has certified in writing to the Red Flag commander that his people are cleared to go that low, according to standard step-down training guidelines. (Times over target can also be compressed during the second week.)

Even a 100-foot altitude is considered stratospheric by some attack pilots; British Tornado crews, for example, spend most of their flying careers below that level. The Brits used to come to Red Flag in a breathtakingly ugly strike jet called the Buccaneer. On one memorable Blue strike, a Buc managed to clip some telephone wires while climbing away from a strafing run. Repair crews reported later that the wires were exactly 42 feet AGL!

B. Mission will be briefed IAW, TACR, 51-2 if a DACT sortie.

These are routine Air Force regulations and guidelines and standard dissimilar rules of engagement. As one pilot has written, "These rules have not been formulated as just another step in the aircrew harassment program, but have been developed as common sense guidelines to insure the safe conduct of the mission." That is, they are the best compromise so far between realism and safety. The rules are common not only throughout the Air Force, but in the Navy, Marine Corps, and Canadian Armed Forces as well. Other friendly air forces, many of which attend Red Flags, fly by similar sets of rules.

2. Rules of Engagement:

A. The Defender must assume an aircraft chasing him into the sun has lost visual contact and he is responsible for maintaining separation.

There are two problems with this particular rule. In the first place, it doesn't make much sense in terms of combat realism. Since the days of the Red Baron, pilots have used the sun to hide in while attacking and defending, primarily because the sun's glare is just as hard to deal with now as it was in 1916. Also, with heat-seeking missiles, defenders often use the sun's heat to distract the infrared seeker heads. When a weak fighter or attack jet finds itself tussling with something like an F-15, it may have no choice other than to drag the superior plane into the sun in hope that the pilot will lose visual contact in the glare.

The second problem with the rule is that it makes the defender responsible for maintaining separation. This makes sense, because the whole point of taking an attacker into the sun is to try to make him lose sight. But the defender doesn't always know when the attacker has lost visual contact, and even a jet with excellent rearward visibility won't always have an eyeball on the bad guy (expecially if the attacker is lurking in the low or deep six o'clock position). In addition, it's possible to take someone into the sun without realizing it. So in most cases now, the rule is that the defender going into the sun must endeavor to maintain a "predictable" flight path, and if the attacker loses visual contact he will clear off to the right.

B. If visual contact is lost during setups for engagements, the flight leader will assure that altitude separation is provided until Tally-ho.

This is part of the "contract," an agreement between the pilots, either briefed before the flight or understood from long experience of flying together. It's important that safe separation altitudes be briefed beforehand because for the rule to take effect, obviously, the opponents can't see each other; neither one knows at that moment what a safe separation altitude is. The problem gets stickier when the two sides are up on different radio frequencies, as they almost always are. This enhances realism, but introduces a time lag between the

Canadian Hornet drivers walk in after kicking serious Red Force butt at Maple Flag in Alberta. John McQuarrie

91

moment the no-visual call is made and when it is passed.

C. If two aircraft approach head-on, each fighter will clear to the right and the fighter with the higher nose position will attempt to go above the opponent.

This is often paraphrased as "nose high goes high." The most dangerous situation develops when two turning aircraft meet head-on under conditions of high positive g. Reaction time is cut drastically short, and the nose-high jet will have to load up like crazy to clear above the opponent. But the rule still applies.

D. Front-quarter gun attacks are not authorized.

This is another example where realism has been sacrificed for safety. And rightly so: with closure rates up around Mach 2 possible, the Nellis range is no place to play chicken. But front-quarter gun attacks would be common in wartime. Phantom drivers used to love head-on passes; when fighting jets that turned better, a fast and close-in pass would make it hard for the opponent to turn and convert on the F-4's tail. The Soviets were always fond of head-on gun passes, and there are still lots of Russian-trained surrogates around the globe. Most Russian jets carry heavier gun armament than Western fighters, and their slow-firing cannons are better employed in frontal attacks.

Some front-quarter gunshots are allowed at Red Flag. When A-10s are in the war, they are permitted to try for gun solutions with their huge 30mm GAU-8 antitank gun, but even they must break things off at 1,000 feet. Warthog crews had always been curious about what their monster gun could do to a fast-mover; they found out in the Gulf, when a Reserve A-10 from the New Orleans-based 962nd Fighter Group Cajuns managed to vaporize an Iraqi BO-105 observation helicopter with a short burst.

In addition, the later versions of the Sidewinder and other European heat-seekers are good for all-aspect shots; amazingly, they are able to pick up enough of an infrared signature to get a lock even from the bad guy's lips. So the traditional six o'clock conversion is no longer necessary, although it's still the most reliable solution. So some face-to-face Sidewinder shots are allowed under the current Red Flag ROE, but with a minimum range of two kilometers. The missiles' minimum ranges are actually much closer.

E. All rear-quarter attacks will be initiated against the trailing wingman in an element. Attacks may be initiated against any element.

The reasoning behind this is that a fighter trying to get behind the lead aircraft runs the risk of a midair collision with the bandit's wingman coming up from the rear. It's a sound tactical move as well because Russian-trained pilots always travel in pairs, although often with such a vast horizontal or altitudinal separation that it's difficult to pick up the trailer—that, of course, is the idea. Cold-eyed aces from the Red Baron to North Vietnam's Colonel Tomb always went for the trailer, not only to avoid being sandwiched but also because the trailer was usually the less-experienced pilot.

On the other hand, if the targets are separated by such distance as to make an attack on the leader possible while preserving enough time and space to defend against the trailer, attacking the leader may be a not-bad idea. "If they're separated by three or more miles," said a Red Flag morning briefer, "be my guest."

At any rate, the terminology of this rule is a bit outdated. Not many air-to-air fighters fight in two-ship elements anymore. The Air Force has moved to the Fluid Two, a two-ship formation with each aircraft effectively taking the part of each two-ship element in the old, Vietnam-era Fluid Four. Also, the notion of a "trailer" is all but extinct. In a Fluid Two, the aircraft may be separated by great horizontal and vertical distances, but they will usually be flying line-abreast. (Nobody wants to be the trailer these days. Trailers get killed.) However, if each aircraft in the Fluid Two is considered an "element," the rule still holds true.

F. Any flight member can terminate the engagement by transmitting "knock it off," at which time all participants will cease maneuvering and acknowledge with call sign.

This rule is expanded somewhat at Red Flag because the Red Flag was, in itself, so expansive. The call to terminate will stop only one small part of the war. For instance, "Terminate the Mirages at Cedar Pass" means someone has noticed something unusual and potentially dangerous concerning the Frenchies over a particular geographic area. The pilot who made the call gives his call sign, and the order is passed over another frequency to the Mirages. The only person who can now restart the battle is the pilot who made the call in the first place. He will do this by saying, "Fight's on at Cedar Pass," (not "Knock it on at Cedar Pass," a phrase popular for a while but now recognized as an effront to both safety and the English language).

To stop the entire war, the pilot calls, "Red Flag, knock it off!" This is the big one, and it means that something terribly wrong has happened. On a Red Flag knock-it-off call, all participants shut up on the radio, roll wings level, turn up the volume on Guard, and go to altitude to look for parachutes.

G. Fighters conducting separate attacks will maintain a minimum of 1,000 feet altitude separation on any target until Tally-ho. All aircraft will have this altitude separation within ten nautical miles. Fighters may transit target area beyond six nautical miles.

This is the altitude block. Combined with the 1,000-foot horizontal separation, it effectively isolates every participating aircraft in a bubble at least 1,000 feet in diameter. This works on paper. But in the sky, in the heat of practice combat, it's sometimes difficult to know—or care—if a pilot is breaking someone else's "bubble." It's a good rule, but difficult to enforce, especially since the pilots involved are the only ones who know when it's violated.

The fighter pilot code of honor precludes ratting on another fighter pilot, unless the other guy is a dangerous flyer, a suicidal lunatic, or a naval aviator. Midair collisions have been rare at Red Flag, but near-misses are not. Remember that there are sometimes eighty planes up for a single battle.

Although 1,000 feet is as close as any aircraft is allowed to come to another aircraft at Red Flag, different aircraft types have different bubbles. Fighters, strikers, bombers, and tactical airlift birds honor the 1,000-foot limitation, while the norm for helicopters is 2,000 feet. And everyone has to keep at least 3,000 feet separation from any of the serious RF emitters—the AWACS, the EA-6B or EF-111A radar jammers, and the EC-130 Hercules that carry either psyops broadcasting stations, communications jammers, or ABCCC (airborne command, control, and communication) modules. In reality no one wants to get anywhere near these guys, for fear of being sterilized or somehow mutated by their enormously powerful microwave emissions.

H. Termination will be accomplished when one of the following situations occurs:

1. If the battle drifts to the border of the authorized area.

This is not as much of a problem at Nellis as it might be at other bases. For one thing, even with all its restrictions, the Nellis ranges are still huge. And there is a Red Flag duty officer monitoring every mission by radar to ensure that pilots don't wander into areas where they don't belong.

2. If an unbriefed, unscheduled flight enters the ACM [Air Combat Maneuvering] work area and is a factor detrimental to the safe conduct of the mission.

Again, since the ranges are so huge and so closely monitored, the bogey—usually some terrified dentist in a Bonanza—is picked up and escorted out of the Red Flag area before he becomes a danger to the participants. Hard as it may be to believe, it is legal and permissible for private civilian aircraft to transit MOAs (Military Operating Areas). But most private pilots in the know—particularly those with any military flying background—won't go anywhere near active MOAs. It's a tempting shortcut for a pilot flying his plane from, say, San Francisco to Albuquerque. But it's a really bad idea.

3. If visual contact is lost by the attacking aircraft within one nautical mile and converging vectors exist, or safe separation cannot otherwise be assured.

You'd think it would be impossible to lose sight of your dogfighting opponent at distances inside a mile. That's what every young tiger thinks before his first tussles with the Adversary Tactics guys. A fighter the size of the F-16 is pretty hard to spot nose-on at any range. Back when the Aggressors flew the tiny F-5E Tiger, fighter pilots used to duking it out with the likes of the Phantom and Tomcat had a terrible time keeping an eyeball on the Gomers.

In peacetime training, the procedure is to signal lost sight as well as current altitude, and turn away from the bandit's last known position. In combat, of course, this could prove fatal. This is where good radar technique comes in. A radar lock would at least give the pilot a clue about which section of the sky to search. The modern digital radars in the F-16C, F/A-18, and Mirage 2000 are very adept at quick acquisition and lock-on at extremely close ranges.

An Eglin-based F-15C Eagle returns to Nellis as atypical rain clouds build over the Nevada desert.
George Hall

94

4. When the desired learning objective is achieved.

Disengagement can be dangerous, even in training. The standard separation for DACT consists of transmitting the call sign and acknowledging the knock-it-off call, selecting military power (the highest throttle setting this side of afterburner) and climbing back to starting altitude.

5. If stalemate occurs.

Fights without a clear initial winner usually degenerate into low-and-slow "knife fights" where nothing is learned except which pilots can turn down the wick the most without losing control. Fighter pilots hate to give it up or call a draw. This sort of slow-speed Russian roulette is called "pride maneuvers," and used to kill pilots in unauthorized hassling. There is no excuse for it now, and pilots have become mature enough to realize the surest way to go back to flying "flagpole missions" is to kill each other in supersonic (or ultra-slow) games of chicken.

6. If any aircraft rocks its wings.

This is the universal signal for NORDO, meaning the aircraft has lost radio communications for some reason. Wing-rocking has been expanded at Red Flag to include all instances where a pilot doesn't want to fight—low fuel, loss of SA (the all-important situational awareness), or mechanical troubles. The wing-rock serves to acknowledge that the pilot sees and recognizes the attacker but doesn't want to come out and play. Usually a squadron-mate will join on a wing and escort the rocker back to base, communicating for both planes if necessary.

7. If bingo fuel is reached.

"Bingo fuel" is the amount needed to return to base with a safe pattern reserve. Most fights or strikes will knock it off at "joker fuel," which includes the added juice needed to effect a valid separation. Joker is much higher than bingo fuel because most separation maneuvers require the use of afterburner, which can raise fuel consumption by a factor of ten. The fuel state at which the fight is called off depends on what type of training is attempted. The im-portant thing is to remain constantly aware of fuel state and make it a realistic part of the training scenario. Some modern jets, most notably the F/A-18 Hornet, seem to be almost out of gas from the moment they take off. Hornet drivers think about fuel a lot.

8. If a dangerous situation is developing.

This is, of course, a judgment call, so we'll let a DACT professional do the talking: "You can recognize from the way the guy's flying his airplane if he's exceeding the safe limits, particularly if he's close to the ground—that's a big threat. That's what we demand of these guys, to have the maturity to say 'knock it off.' We'll set the whole thing up again, and we'll do it right, but we'll do it within these bounds. And if somebody gets himself outside those bounds, we'll stop it. And we'll come down and talk about it in the debrief."

9. If minimum altitude or clouds are approached.

Putting minimum altitude aside for a moment, this is not a rule that helps simulate combat. Clouds, like the sun, can often be a combat pilot's best friend: they help to hide him from attackers and they can mask his engine heat to frustrate an infrared missile shot. But following another aircraft into the clouds where neither pilot can see the other is an excellent way to get killed in a midair—an outcome inappropriate to a peacetime training mission.

10. If radio failure occurs.

11. If communications deteriorate to a point that individual aircraft cannot receive all radio transmissions pertinent to the engagement.

These two rules mean the same thing to varying degrees and point out one of the differences between regular DACT and Red Flag. Certainly in peacetime it's a good idea to knock it off if you can't talk to the ground, your wingman, or the AWACS. But since Red Flag simulates war, and war these days means communications jamming, aircrew must learn to work around it or stay home.

"When we turn on the comm jammers, we go to roll their socks down," says a Red Flag officer. "We want them to know that when it's on, it's on." A setup like the EC-130 Compass Call has awesome power. You can have a wingman fifty feet away and you'll be reduced to hand signals. So anyone in Red Flag who gives up and goes home when his radio doesn't seem to work will be hooted out of the Nellis officers' club for the rest of his life.

Since Red Flag has air-to-ground components that are actually more significant than air-to-air (and all in the same airspace) there are a couple of low-altitude rules added to the regular DACT ROE.

I. Attacks on aircraft below 5,000 feet AGL are authorized with the following limitations:

1. Attackers: The attack may commence from above or below 5,000 feet AGL and will terminate no later than minimum gun range if any member of the flight acknowledges the attack or if the attack flight begins weapons delivery.

This remains a touchy subject at Red Flag. Aircraft concentrating on ordnance delivery have historically been vulnerable; think back on the Eighth Air Force over World War II Germany. At Nellis the danger is extreme because on many of the Red Flag missions, the strikers are dropping live bombs. It's a delicate situation for both the strike aircraft and the attacker since at "minimum gun range" the attacker stands an excellent chance of being fragged by the exploding bombs or ingesting debris into the jet intakes. A 2,000-pound bomb can throw desert dust and hot steel a half mile or more. This is why ground attackers on final weapons deliveries are left alone at Red Flag.

2. Defenders will acknowledge the attack by a radio transmission (if the same frequency), a wing-rock, a level, climbing, defensive turn with a wing-rock, and a return to course (defensive turns not to exceed ninety degrees). Defenders will not maneuver counteroffensively against an attack below 5,000 feet AGL.

The attackers have to be left alone on final weapons delivery, but on the way there and back they are fair game. The Adversary Tactics boys and their henchmen have developed a knack for loitering around the strikers and bouncing them after they pull off the targets. This is perfectly okay, and it's good training for combat. In Vietnam a number of F-105s were shot down as they pulled up after dropping bombs. It's a psychological phenomenon—the pilots, so intent on getting to the target and dropping their loads in narrow parameters, tend to let up after the ordnance is away. And if Red Flag teaches the pilots anything, it is the virtue of paranoia.

The part about not maneuvering counteroffensively sometimes hacks the air-to-ground pilots, particularly the F-16 and F-15E guys, who can flick a switch and revert instantly to fangs-out dogfight mode. These guys look at bombing runs as excuses to sucker bandits into air-to-air engagements. But, in general, it's a good rule because there are so many aircraft at Red Flag, many loaded with the live stuff, and that is not worth the risk. Once again, combat is a whole 'nother thing.

Other missions might have slight changes in the ROE, but this set of rules is pretty close to the one under which most DACT missions are carried out.

Because Red Flag is a unique program, it has unique rules. Chances are a combat pilot will never see more aircraft flying more different missions in one chunk of sky, until *Desert Storm: The Sequel* hits the theaters. As one Red Flag scheduler puts it, "The more jets you have, the more rules you have." Here are some further restrictions that tend to make Red Flag less than realistic in the eyes of some pilots.

First, of course, there is the Nellis range complex itself. It would seem at first glance that with ten million acres to zoom around in, the Players wouldn't be cramped for space.

Well, look again. More than half the range space is devoted to Military Operating Areas. These are valuable slices of airspace in which fighters can zoom around supersonically above a certain level. They are nice to have (the Air Force has never had a decent-size MOA over western Europe), but they are still restrictive. You can't drop bombs in an MOA—civilians live there. And, as mentioned, there's also the occasional ying-yang motoring through in his Cessna. So very little of the Red Flag war takes place there. All the Nellis-controlled MOAs are east of Student Gap, in the no-play area forbidden to adversary aircraft.

The big kicker on the Nellis range is the so-called Dreamland rectangle in the dead center of everything. Various super-secret activities, including US Department of Energy nuclear tests, are conducted in this area, and Red Flag pilots can't even think about entering this black hole. The adjacent Coyote Alpha spaces used to be restricted as well, but they are now open for some activities.

By themselves these space limitations wouldn't be so bad. But the altitude deconfliction rule—the 1,000 foot bubble mentioned earlier—means the mission package going in must be careful not to get too close to the mission package coming out. They do this by staying on their side of the "3740 line," the northern border of the R-74 range. The usual rule is "north in, south out." Sometimes it's the opposite, but for safety reasons it's always predictable. And it's good discipline, although a bit unrealistic due to the narrowness of the Student Gap corridor. General Horner mentioned with pleasure the fact that in several hundred thousand Desert Storm sorties, with hundreds of jets trucking in and out of the combat zones at all hours, there wasn't a single midair collision.

The only other choice is deconfliction by altitude, but since most of the Blue planes want to fly as low as they can to sneak in under the radar and hide from the defenders, deconfliction by altitude is only a semi-viable choice. "It's the kind of thing you can get away with once in a row," says one Player.

Add to Dreamland and the 3740 line the restrictions that prohibit flying with live ordnance over the parts of the electronic warfare ranges where people operate the threat radars. Then it's easy to understand why pilots sometimes complain that their options are severely restricted by the Nellis realities, that tactical innovations—touted by Air Force brass as one of the main reasons for the program—are hard to come by under conditions that force them to be predictable. The rap, in short, is that because of the range restrictions, Red Flag battles end up "canned."

"Everything is concentrated in one little area," says a Wild Weasel pilot. "It's not spread out the way a modern desert battlefield would be."

"Same thing day after day," says a naval aviator flying with the opposition forces. "There's not much flexibility in getting to the attackers."

"The missions end up—I won't say canned—but it's kind of predictable in that you've only got a certain airspace up there that you can run in," says one of the Adversary pilots. "You have the targets here, you've got the entry point here, and there's a little corridor that everybody has to go through to get there."

A past Red Flag commander says he agrees, but that's all right: "It's a big airspace that gets small in a hurry. There are airplanes everywhere all the time. That's good—I want the war to happen."

And he says even the range restrictions are quite realistic: "This is a little bitty slice of a big war. In wartime you're going to have a zone that you're cleared into because there will be zones on your left and right where other aircraft will be working, where other battles are being fought."

As in any game, there are Players at Red Flag who think the rules and the officiating are slanted against them. Some Blue pilots complain about the Adversaries being steered to them by ground controllers, for instance. This way of doing things emulates common Russian tactics. It also dates from the days, only a few years back, when the Nellis Agressors flew the F-5E Tiger, a modest little fighter with no on-board radar, no aerial refueling capability, and only enough gas to play over the range for about twenty minutes. These guys didn't have either the equipment or the gas to go looking for the Blue forces; if they weren't told where to look, there would be no fight and no training. Nowadays the F-16 defenders start off with a drink from the tanker, and they carry good digital radar sets. But they're still steered around by their own ground controllers for much of the battle. Sometimes the comm jammers shut those links down. And sometimes the Adversaries fly more autonomously just for the fun of it; new Russian fighters like the MiG-29 Fulcrum and the Su-27 Flanker have very competitive radar systems, and it's reasonable to assume that their pilots will rely less and less on being told exactly what to do.

Besides, the Blue boys haven't much to complain about since they're getting vectors and helpful hints of their own from the AWACS controllers. And the Adversaries whine about those damned wish-you-were-dead BVR (Beyond Visual Range) missiles like the Sparrow, which often knock them out of the fight before they ever see another jet on the radar.

The officials on the ground call the kills, but again realism suffers. After all, missiles can be spoofed and outmaneuvered. And the for-real Sparrow, in particular, leaves a huge white smoke trail that's impossible to miss.

Pilots in Vietnam used to shoot them at enemy formations even without a good radar lock, just to scatter the Gomers and make them wet their pants. (In those days the Sparrow was notoriously unreliable and, in the opinion of many, not much good for anything else.) And for that matter, a fair number of antiaircraft missiles simply fail to guide for one reason or another. Jets that carry a lot of them (the F-15 can carry four each of the Sparrow and Sidewinder, and the Navy's F-14D Tomcat can be configured to lug twelve AMRAAMS) often take a double shot at any decent target, the second missile following the first by five seconds.

Despite all the I-shot-you-no-I-shot-you-first problems, every pilot with Red Flag experience agrees that realistic air combat training has come a long way since Vietnam. But there are those who say it still doesn't go far enough, that the trade-offs still favor safety too much at the expense of realism. They cite the words of the Navy's only Vietnam ace pilot (and current congressman) Randy "Duke" Cunningham: "You fight like you train."

The Israelis train so that their pilots won't be called upon to do anything in combat (except kill enemies) that they haven't already practiced in peacetime. Hence very few restrictions—no altitude blocks, no bubbles, no whites-of-their-eyes IDs before shooting. It's more dangerous, of course.

"But," says a former Aggressor CO, "the Israelis have a whole different motivation, with all those bad guys right across the street. They're also not dealing with any enemies that are anywhere as well trained as they are."

Do the Israelis have Adversary squadrons and their own Red Flags? "No, they don't," he laughs. "They don't particularly need 'em."

The Israeli Air Force (IAF) may be a bad choice, poised as it is on the brink of war. The British Royal Air Force (RAF) and Royal Navy (RN) pilots train with fewer constraints, and they tend to chafe somewhat under the added restrictions when they come to play at Red Flag.

The Red Flag commanders don't worry much about the complaints, though. The program is what you make it, they say, and besides, for the newcomer, the Nellis range in mock wartime is dangerous enough. Red Flag exists to give the new jocks their first ten combat missions; anything else is gravy. They want to train him, not overwhelm him. They want to put him under lots of pressure, not into a smoking hole in the desert. As the local saying goes, they don't want to see him "going into real estate north of Las Vegas." The rules are there to keep the young pilots from dying trying. In that respect, a former Red Flag CO thinks they're getting the perfect balance.

"You always run a risk in aviation," he says of the pilots who come to Red Flag for the first time. "You want a young, aggressive man,

A communications-jamming EC-130 Compass Call Hercules, based at Tucson's Davis-Monthan AFB, *lifts out of Nellis on a Red Flag 92-4 mission.* George Hall

a twenty-three-year-old with a forty-year-old's maturity and skill. That's asking a lot. You have to be careful to keep the aggressiveness because it's essential to the business. But you also have to have the maturity to recognize the limits and the value of your equipment."

"So it's a fine balance," the CO continues, "flying the airplane to the maximum capability, but not bashing it here, because you're not hurting anybody but us. It can be done. But you've got to do it safely. And you have to fly shit-hot."

Eagles CAP the strike packages from high altitude,
where their immensely powerful radars are at their
most efficient. George Hall

Chapter 6

30 Minutes Over Tonopah

So what's it like to fly in Red Flag? Most of us will never know. Few civilians get to ride along on real Red Flag missions; the intent here is to take the reader along on a typical one, seen Rashoman-like through many eyes. These little glimpses are reconstructions from aircrew interviews and flights followed on the Red Flag Measuring and Debriefing System (RFMDS) computer displays. Although real enough in detail, some of the events may have happened on different missions, and in that sense this little half-hour over the range is, to use the intel folks' favorite phrase, "completely notional."

ENKO 71: Tanker Track AR 625

Red Flag operates its own Tanker Task Force to provide a pre-strike shot of JP-5 to anyone who might need it. The tankers deploy to the task force from around the country, just as the Players do. Three refuelers, either KC-135s or the larger KC-10s, get airborne for each fight. Two take care of the Blue forces in track AR (Aerial Refueling) 641 east of the range, and the third gases the Red fighters in AR 625 on the west side.

The tankers stage out of Beale AFB, the northern California base famous until recently as the home of the SR-71 Blackbird. Nowadays it hosts the weird, glider-like U-2 and TR-1 recon jets, plus a lot of tankers. ENKO 71 is a KC-135R based at Altus AFB, Okla-homa; its crew is deployed for two weeks' worth of Red Flag gas-passing.

The R-model, re-engined with super-efficient Snecma CFM-56 turbofans, climbs out of Beale at a fighter-like pitch angle, despite the ninety-eight-degree heat and the 150,000 pounds of gas on board. Forty minutes later and five minutes late into track 625, the tanker finds its gaggle of receivers waiting impatiently.

First onto the pipe are the fighters of FAZER flight, four F-16Cs out of Luke AFB. Each is on and off the boom in four minutes apiece, full of gas and ready to jump the Blue strikers. Waiting at four o'clock and a half mile is a Thunderbirds-tight echelon of four more C-models. This is MIG flight, the Red Flag adversary pilots, in four identical Fulcrum paint jobs.

MIG flight takes the same four minutes each, and then it's over. All eight adversaries streak to the fight, about two minutes behind where they'd like to be. After a single call-in from FAZER lead, the entire refueling evolution had been accomplished without a word on the radio. Now we hear them trading a few words on their frequency, and then they're "in hot." Some Blue bombers are going to have a lousy day.

The tanker's navigator, listening to the whole ugly spectacle on a BLACKJACK frequency, reports later that "everybody died

A Navy F-14 Tomcat RIO's view of aerial refueling from a drogue-configured Air Force KC-135 in the Red tanker track. Tom Twomey

A tanker boom operator, reclining on his stomach in the rear of his KC-135, scans aft for his expected receivers. George Hall

about four times over." We try to eavesdrop on the Red freq from the boomer's position, but Compass Call pays a visit on the channel. The comm-jamming EC-130 completely obliterates all talk on the Red freq, forcing the bad-guy fighters to think and act without the link to their Russian-style ground controllers.

With the fight over, the Compass Call Herk calls to request a couple of practice plugs and maybe 15,000 pounds of fuel. We vector them in, and in a few minutes COMM 31 is back in the pre-contact position with receiving port open. Fighters often ask the tanker to "push it up," referring to higher airspeed. COMM 31 wants us to "pull it back," as the turboprop Herk is having some trouble keeping up. Its vertical tail is festooned with a rhomboid network of antenna wires, from which a constant stream of high-RF banshee jamming had been emanating a few minutes before. Our boomer asks the Compass Call to double-check that all transmitters are shut down before coming under the boom. "Millions of watts," he says. "The AWACS too, and the EF-111 'Spark Vark.' Can't be anywhere near those things when they're radiating—not when you're sitting on top of this much gas."

RATCH Flight: Gold Flat

Up and down. Up and down. Fighter pilots don't mind all the positive gs in the world. It's the *negative* gs, the kind that lift you up out of your seat on the roller coaster, that are especially uncomfortable. Fighter pilots may hate 'em, but the attack guys love 'em.

RATCH 33 is an F-111 Aardvark, fast and low over the sizzling desert. The terrain-following radar guides the huge jet over the jagged ridges. The two-person crew has dialed in max hard ride, full-macho tactical, and the plane hawks up and down like a crazy elevator with them in it, banging around like dice in a cup.

That's the trouble with Red Flag, to say nothing of the real thing—you can't merely hit

RATCH 33 pitches up over Tolicha airfield with a full load of live Mark 82 500-pounders. George Hall

103

your target, you have to survive as well. RATCH 33 is trying everything in the trick bag: low-level yanking and cranking, defensive ECM from the on-board jammer, chaff, flares, groveling in the weeds like a craven rodent, you name it. And it works; all bombs on target, no good threat lock-ups.

HAZER 02: Pahute Mesa

The tactical reconnaissance mission is about the only thing that gets the Phantom an invite to Red Flag anymore. The Navy and Marine Corps have totally phased out the magnificent old F-4, and the Air Force isn't far behind. The Air National Guard will still be flying the RF-4C as a recon jet for another couple of years, and one Guard outfit has taken over the active Air Force's Wild Weasel mission for the G-model. Otherwise, it's pharewell to the Phantom.

HAZER 02 is down for a couple of weeks from his base at Reno airport. He and his wingman are with the 152nd Reconnaissance Group, the High Rollers, and his jet for the day, the beautifully maintained serial number 65-886, is a veteran of both Vietnam and Persian Gulf duty. How many Red Flag birds can make that statement?

He's got the snapshots, and he's heading out of the range on the deck and at the speed of heat. It's a Phantom feat few modern jets can match: Mach 1.2 at sea level. The desert is just a brown blur, the landscape washing around the Phantom's camera-stuffed nose like waves around the prow of a ship. He's going so fast, in fact, that the scene he sees through the canopy bow is actually a picture of what he's already passed!

Nobody catches the Rhino at this speed, so the pilot kicks back a bit to enjoy a couple minutes' worth of supersonic cruise control. Only one problem: he's picked up a wise-guy

Air National Guard RF-4C recon Phantoms blast out of Nellis as only Phantoms can. These jets are among the few that are veterans of both Vietnam and Desert Storm. Dan McGee

adversary F-16, who's cheerfully hanging at eight o'clock and matching his moves! These things aren't possible! Actually, that's mostly true: the Falcon has ramped down from way above, and he can't keep up for more than a few seconds, even in full burner. The Gomer gives the recce boys a little wave as he falls back—a friendly reminder that you're never safe out here in Redland, no matter what you may think.

HUD Flight: Worthington Peak

Here comes the Wall of Eagles!

The four Holloman F-15s are line abreast, a mile apart, 30,000 feet above a jagged escarpment called the Dinosaur. They're not hiding from anyone. It's impossible to hide an Eagle, anyway; they call it the "aluminum overcast" or the "twin-tailed tennis court." Everyone knows who they are and what they're up to. Spread out across the sky, scanning the range with their powerful radar, the wall makes it harder for anyone to sneak up behind them. And when they get to the free-fire zone, the areas in the west where the visual ID rules are suspended, they can start throwing Sparrows around, confident that whoever's out there isn't "one of us." All the Blue strikers, from B-1s down to the little Falcons, have blown through and done their

A recon Phantom of the 152nd Reconnaissance Group, the High Rollers, at the speed of heat over the Nellis range. Recon jets are armed only with *their great speed; their credo is "one pass and haul ass." Dan McGee*

A four-ship "wall of Eagles" taking part in a late-1980s Red Flag exercise. George Hall

worst. And the Guard RF-4s whipped through eight minutes ago, an eternity on the range; as the recce pukes say, "one pass and haul ass."

The Wall of Eagles is a macho scare tactic, a balls maneuver. It says, Come on out and fight, you worthless Gomer devils! Hit us with your best shot!

Of course, it would work best on real Gomers, not on adversary Falcons piloted by former Aggressor drivers who are just a wee bit harder to psych out. HUD 01 picks up a couple of F-16s on the radar, down low, and two a few miles back, higher. The old Kuban shelf tactic again. He locks up one bandit for

Where did he come from? A Strike Eagle lights burners in an unsuccessful effort to evade an attacking Red Force F-15. The latter is in perfect gun-tracking parameters. George Hall

an AIM-7 (Sparrow) shot, while the other one—disappears? Wait a minute! Gone, just like that. Wiped right off the screen.

This is not the Romulan cloak of invisibility, merely a nicely executed zero-Doppler turn. It's a sure sign that this guy cut his Aggressor teeth with the F-5 in the late-lamented 64th and 65th Squadrons. The F-15's digital Doppler radar needs movement for a good lock; turn just right and the radar will think you've stopped dead. Russian air show pilots have been showing off tail-slide and "cobra" maneuvers that really do stop the jet dead in the sky for a moment. Then turn head-on into the Eagle, and his radar will have trouble with that too.

The Wild Weasel SAM-suppression mission is still being handled by the F-4G Phantom, although the Air Force is experimenting with variations of the F-16 and F-15 to take over the job from the aging birds. George Hall

A Red Force controller runs his side of the fight from a corner of the BLACKJACK control facility. George Hall

Anyway, HUD 01 calls a Sparrow shot, waits five seconds, and calls another Fox 1. So much for the Gomer lead. Now where the hell did that other clown go?

WEASEL Flight: Mount Helen

They *were* an arrow, a twenty-five-ton projectile headed for the heart of Kawich Valley. Now they are low, level, and lurching across the desert floor, building energy for the Big Move coming up. The pilot jerks back on the stick; behind him the Electronic Warfare Officer or EWO (called the Bear in the Weasel world) feels the gs dig in as the nose of the F-4G points at the sky over Belted Peak.

Along with tactical reconnaissance, the Wild Weasels are the only other knuckleheads

A McDonnell Douglas F-15E Strike Eagle is a beefed-up version of the Eagle two-seater with state-of-the-art systems for precision bombing in any weather. The jet was employed with great success throughout Desert Storm. George Hall

110

who bring the much-loved Phantom to Red Flag these days. As of this writing the mission is being given to a former Air National Guard recce outfit in Boise, Idaho, and they can be expected to flog the honored Weasel tradition for a few more years. The active Air Force is planning on using Falcons or Strike Eagles to do the job, but somehow it won't be quite the same.

Wild Weasels regularly join the good guys in both Red Flag and electrified Green Flag exercises. The job is tricky, dangerous, and all-important. Go in ahead of the strikers and do what *real* wild weasels supposedly do: use yourself for bait. Hopefully, you'll get the enemy to lock you up with his ground-to-air SAM and AAA radars. When he does, you do two things: first, record his location electronically and squirt his fingerprint via data-link to the AWACS; second, blow him to smithereens with a SHRIKE or HARM antiradiation missile, horrid little Kamikazes that literally fly right down his radar beam. He may recognize you and shut off his gear in a panic, but it will be too late. His location will remain frozen on the Bear's back-seat scopes. And even if he doesn't take a hit, he and his antiair weapons will have been neutralized successfully if you can simply terrify him into turning off the electrons.

As the jet pulls vertical above Kawich, the Bear lifts up his seventy-pound head and

Aircrews of French Armee de l' Aire with the Mirage 2000s at Red Flag 92-4. George Hall

thumps it against the shield around the main scope. The glare from the sun is tremendous—straight above them now, washing the cockpit in white light. He strains his neck and eyes, peering into the screens, waiting for the inevitable. And there it is: the CRTs flash and sparkle like the Vegas Strip itself, each point of light representing not a kinder and gentler Redland but a mortal danger on the ground.

Then the screens go blank. The threat guys have recognized the blip on *their* scope for what it is, a threat to them rather than a target. They've shut down their transmitters, but it's too late. Their images and locations are frozen in green phosphorescence on the EWO's scopes. The whole package will be briefed on the threat locations before tomorrow's go.

The Weasels hit the floor again, the pair of them arcing like dolphins. They take turns keeping the sites covered. The SAM operators have shut down for good, it seems. Just like those weasels in human form working the systems in Iraq—nary a peep out of them after the first few days of the air war. The Weasels in the Gulf flew three weeks' worth of boring, uneventful missions, trying like crazy to tempt some idiot into painting them. That's the great thing about the Weasel mission: blow 'em up or turn 'em off, and it's a successful hop either way.

MIG Controllers: Range Control Center

"MIG 11, I have one contact just coming down the ridgeline over Pahute Mesa. Target

The Dassault Mirage 2000 is a current-technology warplane with tremendous power, fly-by-wire flight *controls, and excellent software for its radar weapons.* Katsuhiko Tokunaga

113

heading southwest—that should be a Weasel bearing about three-six-zero for six miles from FLOGGER.

"I've got a flight of four Eagles over Worthington Peak—they're showing westbound now at Angels 27.

"Okay, the Eagles have split into deuces at 27 and 30, going 090. I've got somebody just north of FLOGGER—looks like one of the Weasels just north of FLOGGER at about, ah, six thousand.

"Big strike gaggle crossing Coyote at six thousand due west; I've got Eagles at thirty thousand over Worthington Peak, looks like they're starting to turn southwest now—all contacts are on the western part of Pahute Mesa at this time.

"FLOGGER, the only contacts I have in your area are something two-three-zero for ten miles.

"Okay, MIG, the Eagles are zero-three-zero for twenty-two miles southwest bound, pointing right at you at Angels 30.

"MIG, from you estimate the Eagles about zero-three-zero for twenty.

"I have a contact on the Eagles now at zero-two-zero from MIG, no, correction, from me. There's a four-ship wall coming at you, now showing Angels 22 for sixteen miles. Don't say I didn't warn you."

An Air National Guard C-130 down low in the Nellis MOA. Farming and residences are permitted in the operating areas, but life on the ground is a nightmare during Red Flag evolutions. George Hall

MIG Flight: Quartzite Mountain

Cruising in from the tanker as the second tier of the old Russian Kuban Steppe (*Kubanskaya Etazherka)* formation, MIG 11 is extremely ticked off to hear that he has been shot down. He hasn't even seen an Eagle! Nowhere near the fight, and he hears a radio call: "Fox 1 kill on the bandit over Quartzite."

He is incensed, but hardly surprised: this sort of thing happens all the time when they show up late from the tanker and the Eagles catch them over the free-fire zone. He cranks the F-16 around, and he and his wingman head back to Cedar Pass, their regeneration point. He's mad now, but wait till he finds out that four more Eagles have capped the regeneration point too!

HARLY 22: Kawich Valley

The pilot of the F-15E Strike Eagle (an unofficial name the crews like a lot, but the Air Force wants us all to call it the Dual Role Eagle) thinks he sees a glint back behind the port wing, about eight o'clock. He can't worry about it right now; he's lined up for his pop-up delivery, and he's a lot more concerned about

Herk pilots study complex ingress routes to various dry lakebed landing areas on the Nellis ranges.
George Hall

live ordnance than he is about pretend MiGs. Maybe it's not the best training, but it's the safest. At the top of his pull-up, he rolls the big jet 180 and heads upside down for the desert floor. The target is a fairly realistic Scud launcher, cleverly pieced together from cinder blocks and a B-52 drop tank. It's still enshrouded in desert dust from the pounding the other strikers have administered.

HARLY computer-pickles his iron bombs, lights the pipes, and blasts out energy-rich. He won't know until later about his bombing score, but he knows right away that he's been had big-time: the Weapons Systems Officer (WSO) in the back seat calls out one of those Fulcrum-painted F-16s in perfect AA-10 parameters.

That's the trouble with the one-seat Eagle escorts—they're never around when you need them.

PARLAY Flight: Sun Valley

Hey, this is fun! Dust-ups like this are hard to arrange in the ultra-crowded airspace

A portable gun loader puts over 1,000 rounds into an A-10's nose-mounted GAU-8 cannon on dry Texas Lake. Hogs can take on gas and a full gun load in ten minutes. George Hall

over western Europe. France's Armee de L'Air has sent eight of its state-of-the-art Mirage 2000s to the fight, and four of them are blowing back to Nellis in a tight *apres* combat echelon. Two of the jets are blue single-seat C-models, the air-superiority fighter version. The other two are desert-camouflage K-models, two-person strike bombers with navigator-bombardiers in back.

In a flashy show of French versatility, all four jets have scored bulls-eyes with iron bombs (the fighters have hard points for bombs, although they don't often use them), and the two-seat strikers even mixed it up air-to-air with some hassling Red Falcons. Every-one in PARLAY flight (as in *parlez-vous*, get it?) took off with a mix of Mark 84s and two Matra Magic heat-seekers apiece, ready to go either way as the battle dictated. The French pilots are proud of their fly-by-wire hummer, the most modern combat craft in their inventory until the awesome Rafale goes into service. They fly it aggressively, skillfully, and with panache.

Just one little problem: they may have hit their targets and smoked a couple of Red defenders, but the threat-meisters on the ground chewed them up something fierce. The Mirages all carry excellent electronic countermeasures suites, but you have to remember to

A "Bone" rolls out from Nellis' newly constructed "heavy pad" for a Red Flag sortie. The big jet is amazingly agile; pilots report that it handles exactly like a big fighter. George Hall

Previous page
A "Bad-to-the-Bone" 3g break over the Nellis runways after a successful Red Flag bomb run. The B-1B begs to be flown like a much smaller jet. Tom Twomey

turn them on! Speed and jinking aren't enough these days. It won't be much fun watching those threat videos.

But hey, *c'est la guerre*. After a lengthy debrief—longer, in fact, than the hop itself—it's off to the Strip for a night on the town. Let's just hope they don't get the idea that Las Vegas is your typical American city.

BEATER 51: Texas Lake

Photographer George Hall manages to bum a ride on an operational Red Flag mission, and lives to tell this tale:

I can't believe I got talked into doing this. I actually did it once before, so there's *really* no excuse for my repeat stupidity. We're low (*very* low), fast, and rough in a C-130 Hercules that journeyed all the way from Rhein-Main Air Base in Germany to make my life a living hell.

Since I've flown in lots of different military types, people often ask me about my least-comfortable flying experience. They expect to hear about some God-awful 9-G dogfight in a psychopathic F-16. I've lived through a few of those, and they're pretty bad, but all-out ACM engagements only last a few minutes, a quarter hour tops. We humans can survive a few minutes of just about anything.

Today's Red Flag mission in the Herk is a bit different. See, it sounded so innocuous: we're just going to fly into a bunch of dry-lake landing fields to simulate dropping supplies, and we're even going to refuel A-10s out on Texas Lake from a hastily installed rubber bladder amidships. We're also packing a portable ammo-loader on wheels that stuffs belts of 30mm rounds into the Warthog's nose.

I was tuning out in the brief when the discussion turned to low-level defensive maneuvering. It seems that some of the Red fighters will be looking to kill us, so we'll have to keep up a constant stream of defensive maneuvers as we fly between each leg of the mission. I move from tuning out to denial when I hear that the mission will last about three hours.

As we enter the range a few minutes after taking off from Nellis, we drop to 300 feet AGL and stay there for the duration, except when we go lower. The big turboprop transport is almost never level, with forty-five-degree banks to one side or the other every few seconds. From my seat behind the pilots I fixate on the g-meter, which alternates monotonously between three-plus and three-minus, spending scarcely an instant at plain old one. Keep your belt fastened, or you'll be gazing down from the ceiling.

During a lull I lurch into the dark, cavernous cargo area and belt myself into a canvas sling seat; maybe I won't get sick if I stop looking out the front windows. Yeah, right. The two crew chiefs are wandering around and busying themselves with their little tasks, seemingly unconcerned with this manic ocean motion. At least the two airmen who came with the gun loader look greener than I do. Well, I hope I don't look that bad.

The three hours is a blur of rough-field landings in a thousand feet, takeoffs in less than a thousand feet, swirling dust in the cabin, 108 degree heat, and terrifying glimpses of desert and mountain through the portholes.

We get a little respite when we land to service the A-10s; the flight crew prop themselves up against the main wheels and break out appetizing box lunches. Yum!

I'm convinced that you could put a three-thousand-hour fighter jock on one of these hops-to-Hades and make him so sick he'll

Next page
The Navy's F-14D is a much-improved Tomcat of the 1990s, with vastly superior powerplants and updated electronics. The big jet is also carving out a role for itself as an all-weather bomber, in the mode of the F-15E Strike Eagle. Tom Twomey

flash back to flight school. Me, I'll choose fighter-type abuse any day—not that any of it is all that enjoyable. Back on the Nellis ramp, the Herksters find great hilarity in my pitiful efforts to walk a straight line. We learn in the debrief that our defensive efforts were semi-successful; the fighters shot us several times over, but they admitted that we were a tougher target than they'd expected. They'd keep misjudging our snap-turns, and they'd overshoot. The moral of this story is simple: if

you ever get invited on a macho tactical Herk ride, Just Say No.

BONE 41: Cedar Pass

It's surprising to see something as big as the B-1B honking across the live ranges so *low* and so *fast*. Few fighters can keep pace with it on the deck; one cherished defensive tactic is to run from attackers. The big jet has been joining Red Flag Blue strikes since 1991, and everyone at Nellis has gotten used to treating

An F-14 Tomcat RIO (Radar Intercept Officer) in the back seat catches a snapshot of the Mach meter as his jet blows past the speed of sound. Supersonic flight is permitted in the MOAs (Military Operating Areas) north of Nellis AFB. Tom Twomey

it as a great big attack jet rather than as a strategic bomber.

BONE 41 is staging out of Nellis with two squadron-mates and another trio of BUFFs (B-52s). The norm used to be long nonstop missions from bases in the Midwest, but the Red Flag planners thought it would make for more realistic training if the former Strategic Air Command (SAC) pukes flew off the Nellis runway like everyone else. And the boys are loving it.

"We're still pissed about being left out of Desert Storm," says one of the pilots from Dyess AFB, Texas. "The jet has had a lot of problems, but it's working well now. It's becoming a very mature weapons system, and it's been totally under-utilized. It's a bitchin' jet for this conventional strike role. And we love our call sign for this Red Flag. The Air Force wants everyone to call this thing the Lancer, but we just call it The Bone."

The nickname, of course, derives from "B-One," but it could just as well mean the "backbone" of the Air Combat Command's newly consituted bomber fleet—a mix of ancient B-52s, all ninety-five B-1Bs, and a possible maximum of twenty B-2s yet to come. Or as in "bad to the bone," with a nod to George Thorogood and the Delaware Destroyers.

Today BONE 41 is trying a new tactic, a high-speed bomb delivery in tight wing-to-wing formation with his squadron-mates. The three bombers (sorry: big attack jets) are doing Mach 0.95 at 400 feet AGL, in line a quarter mile apart. The delivery is timed to the second: simulated today for reasons of economy, but impressive nevertheless. Realize that these three musketeers can deliver eighty-four Mark 82 500-pounders apiece in the space of three seconds. That's sixty-three tons of high-explosive trash on an area target; think how it might have worked on, say, a fleeing Republican Guards division in western Kuwait.

BONE flight blows off to the west with twelve afterburners lit, the escorting fighters working overtime to keep up. B-b-b-bad to the bone.

SQUID 33: Stonewall Airfield

If you think the Eagle is a big fighter, wait till you see this hummer coming at you. The F-14 Tomcat needs its great size to give it the range and weapon-carrying capabilities it must have for its traditional mission, that of long-range fleet defense. But despite its heft, it's a surprisingly agile dogfighter, especially in the new re-engined D version. Getting rid of the weak, balky Pratt and Whitney TF 30s gives the jet an entirely new personality. Great new digital radar and avionics, too.

Today SQUID flight (Red Flag takes great delight in assigning stupid call signs to the Navy) is helping out Red air, playing pure fighter in the crystalline Nevada skies. If 33 and his wingman can sneak around the flank and enter the Blue package from the side, they hope to confuse their identity long enough for a few well-placed Fox 1s (radar-guided Sparrow shots). The rules say no Phoenixes today; the huge missile, peculiar to the Tomcat, has such an amazingly long range that the boys could almost take their shots from down around their base at Miramar.

The Tomcats can do just fine air-to-air, thank you very much. There's that second guy in the back seat, handling the intercepts and putting another pair of eyes to work. And they love to play a trick that's just made to order for Red Flag: crank the variable-sweep wings back about halfway to fifty degrees, turn the computer off so they won't move by themselves as the jet maneuvers, and from five miles they look exactly like a two-ship of F-15Es. Now pitch up from low altitude, as if you're pulling off your bombing run, and voila—complete surprise. Don't you just love it when a plan comes together?

Chapter 7

The Future

The astonishing events of the past few years—the collapse of Communism, the Gulf war, the inevitable downsizing of the American military—have both validated and called into question the Red Flag basics. Potential enemy threats have always ebbed and flowed, but seldom more suddenly and dramatically than in the years since 1988. The prognosticators were sound asleep, it seems; none of the usual experts saw any of these changes and events coming.

Throughout most of Red Flag's history, its architects were concerned that it lacked fundamental applicability to the Big Threat—land war in central Europe. The Maple Flag component at CFB Cold Lake was added to provide a more realistic backdrop—white ground, green trees, cold temperatures, and horrible flying weather. The supreme irony was that Red Flag turned out to be perfect preparation for the air war that actually happened. All informed sources agree that Desert Storm was a whole lot slicker, safer, and more devastating because of the Red Flag experience.

Future Red Flag scenarios will run the gamut. War 92-4 was a Caribbean exercise, with French and Latin American assets joining the United States in a fight with an island despot. The first war of the 1993 season was a Balkan affair, with a US and European coalition trying to sort out the struggles of four republics (formerly one nation) that hate each other. Sound familiar? And coming in the near future: the first Red Flag built around an "armed humanitarian rescue" theme—the kind of problem taken on by the Marines in Somalia, the Philippines, and Bangladesh since 1990.

The possibilities are open-ended. The only thing we're likely *not* to see at Nellis is that chestnut of the early 1980s, the Soviet armored thrust through Germany's Fulda Gap. Recently appointed CIA boss R. James Woolsey said at his confirmation hearing that we've triumphantly slain the enormous Soviet dragon, only to find ourselves ankle-deep in a thousand poisonous snakes. Red Flag will have to continue providing prescient leadership and warfighting know-how, in sync with real-life future threats, if it is to survive and prevail in the austere times ahead.

Tomcat back-seater LT Tom "Tumor" Twomey, USN, grabs a self-portrait as his jet cranks the wings back and grovels in the weeds at 500 knots. Tom Twomey

Glossary

AA-10 Russian radar homing missile; NATO code name Alamo.

AAA Antiaircraft artillery; known in World War II as flak; often radar-directed.

ACM Air Combat Maneuvering.

Afterburner System that blows raw fuel into the hot jet exhaust, thus greatly increasing both thrust and fuel consumption.

AGL Above ground level; atmospheric altimeters read altitude from sea level.

AMRAAM Advanced Medium-Range Air-to-Air Missile, designated AIM-120; capable new replacement for Sparrow radar missile.

AWACS Airborne Warning and Control System; the principal Air Force AWACS is the E-3 Sentry, based on the Boeing 707 airframe.

Bear Nickname for the Electronic Warfare Officer (EWO) in the back seat of the Wild Weasel.

BFM Basic Fighter Maneuvers.

Boomer Tanker crew chief and refueling boom operator.

BVR Beyond Visual Range.

CAVU Clear Air, Visibility Unlimited; the norm at Nellis AFB.

CFB Canadian Forces Base.

Chaff Foil strips dropped by aircraft to confuse radar.

Check Six Refers to the clock system from the pilot's viewpoint: twelve o'clock is dead ahead, six o'clock is dead astern; a common salutation and sign-off among combat pilots.

CO Commanding officer.

DACT Dissimilar Air Combat Training.

ECM Electronic countermeasures.

FAC Forward Air Control; directs ordnance and artillery on target; may be in the air or on the ground.

Fire-and-Forget Refers to a weapon that can be left to its own devices once fired—an artillery shell, a Sidewinder heat-seeker, or an AMRAAM radar missile; the Sparrow is a semi-active radar missile, meaning that the launching aircraft must continue to paint the target with radar energy until the missile arrives, thus the mother aircraft cannot turn away to engage or evade an enemy until the Sparrow impacts.

Flanker, Fulcrum, Flogger NATO code names for Russian fighter aircraft.

Flares These are much like auto flares; they are dropped behind a military aircraft to lure away heat-seeking missiles.

Fox 1, Fox 2, Fox 3 Radio calls for launch of Sparrow, Sidewinder, and Phoenix missile, respectively.

Furball Large multi-aircraft dogfight.

Gomer A flying bad guy.

GPS Global Positioning System; permits accurate determination of location anywhere on earth via geosynchronous satellites.

Grail, Grumble, Gladiator NATO code names for Russian surface-to-air missiles.

Guard Emergency radio channel monitored by all Players; some tend to turn down the volume on Guard to avoid its distractions.

HAWK Homing All the Way Killer; deadly US ground-to-air missile system used by many countries.

Hard Point Mounting station under an aircraft's wing, with standardized hardware for hanging ordnance, fuel tanks, or ECM pods.

HUD Head Up Display.

Hummer Nickname for any ingenious machine in addition to "puppy" and "bad boy"; common nickname also for the HMMWV, the Army's jeep of the 1990s, and for the Navy's E-2C Hawkeye airborne surveillance aircraft.

IAF Israeli Air Force; USAF pilots consider the IAF the only fliers in the world who might be their equals.

IFF Identification, Friend or Foe; electronic transponders that emit signals for positive ID in a combat situation.

INS Inertial Navigation System.

IR Infrared.

Knife Fight A low-speed dogfight that is dangerous and hard to win.

Knot One nautical mile per hour; one knot is about 1.15 statute miles per hour.

LANTIRN Low-Altitude Navigation and Targeting Infrared for Night.

LGB Laser-Guided Bomb; the bomb guides itself to a coded spot of laser light being painted on the target.

Mark 82, Mark 84 Iron "dumb" bombs, weighing 500 pounds and 1,000 pounds, respectively; aircraft like the F-16 and F-15E can place them with tremendous accuracy, even though they can't be guided.

MiG Aircraft of the Mikoyan-Gurevich Design Bureau, premiere Russian aircraft designers.

Mort Dead, as in "I shot you, you're a mort."

No Joy Failure to sight another aircraft.

NORDO No radio communications; signaled by wing-rocking.

Patriot State-of-the-art US surface-to-air missile system.

Phoenix Navy radar-guided air-to-air missile, designated AIM-54; carried only by the F-14 Tomcat; long-range, fire-and-forget, huge warhead.

Poopy Suit Water survival flight gear worn for long trans-ocean flights; usually contains unpleasant-to-use diaper affair for bodily relief.

RAF Royal Air Force; the air arm of the United Kingdom.

RHAW Radar Homing and Warning receiver; an airborne Fuzzbuster that tells pilot that a radar weapon or system is "painting" him.

RN Royal Navy of the United Kingdom.

ROE Rules of Engagement.

Route Pack Six Targeting corridor over Hanoi and Haiphong in the Vietnam War; also known as Downtown.

SA Situational awareness; all-encompassing term for keeping track of what's happening while flying and fighting in a high-performance aircraft; involves knowing what your jet is doing relative to its envelope, where your adversary is and what he's up to, where the ground is, the status of enemy threats on the ground, and a hundred other factors.

SAM Surface-to-air missile; may be heat-seeking or radar-guided.

SEAL Sea-Air-Land; elite, highly trained Navy commandos.

Sidewinder Short-range infrared missile, designated AIM-9.

Sierra Hotel Polite phonetics for "shit-hot," the fighter pilot's all-purpose expression of maximum approval.

Sparrow Medium-range radar homing missile, designated AIM-7; eventually will be replaced by the AMRAAM.

Speed of heat, speed of thought Very, very fast.

Stinger Shoulder-fired US surface-to-air heat-seeker.

Warthog Universal nickname for the A-10 Thunderbolt II.

Whiskey Delta More polite phonetics for "weak dick," a pilot who can't cut it; such a scurrilous term that it's almost never used.

Wingman Second pilot in a two-ship pair; also called dash two.

ZSu-23 Russian-built 23mm antiaircraft artillery piece, commonly nicknamed the Zip Gun.

Index